D1577137

PRACTICAL ELECTRONICS
FOR RAILWAY MODELLERS

PRACTICAL ELECTRONICS
FOR RAILWAY MODELLERS

Roger Amos

 Patrick Stephens, Cambridge

WARNING! ELECTRICITY CAN BE DANGEROUS!
The electronic projects in this book are, to
the best of the author's knowledge and belief,
both accurately described and safe. However,
great care must always be taken when
assembling electronic circuits, and neither the
publishers nor the author can accept
responsibility for any accidents which may
occur.

First published in 1982

British Library Cataloguing in Publication Data

Amos, Roger
   Practical electronics for railway modellers.
   1. Railroads—Models—Electronic equipment
   2. Electronic circuits
   I. Title
   625.1'9'028   TF197

   ISBN 0-85059-555-X

Text photoset in 10 on 11pt English Times by
Manuset Limited, Baldock, Herts.
Printed in Great Britain on white book wove
90 gsm Vol 18, and bound, by The Garden
City Press, Letchworth, for the publishers,
Patrick Stephens Limited, Bar Hill,
Cambridge, CB3 8EL, England.

Contents

Part 4   Train detection systems   54

Part 5   Automatic signalling and turnout (points) control   66

Part 6   Locomotive and coach lighting   96

Introduction

Railway modelling is probably the most broadly based of constructive hobbies. Its interests incorporate not only the essential features of model railway construction and operation, but also the peripherals of scenery modelling and the achievement of precise control of the layout. Railway modellers themselves are as diverse a cross section of the community as any. The range of skills needed to construct a model railway of exhibition standard is vast: the team needs to include a competent carpenter, metalworker, artist, mathematician, railway historian and—almost certainly—electrician. The exclusion clause 'almost certainly' is a concession to the limited number of enthusiasts whose interests are confined to clockwork or live-steam models. The vast majority of model locomotives from N gauge to 0 gauge, whether representing steam-, diesel- or electrically-propelled prototypes are powered by 12V dc motors deriving their power either from the two running rails or from one running rail and overhead catenary.

Although the electrification of a large layout is a complex matter, much has been written about it and the subject is generally well understood by railway modellers. Many an experienced modeller can take the plan of a proposed layout and quickly decide where to insert feeds and rail breaks. This demands a genuine insight into the behaviour of electricity. It is surprising, therefore, that to so many railway modellers the subject of electronics is a 'closed book', since this too deals with the behaviour of electricity. Electronics, however, is concerned primarily with the applications of those devices whose operation involves the control of free electron flow in, for example, semi-conducting material. Such devices include semi-conductor diodes, (bipolar) transistors and field-effect transistors. Integrated circuits or 'silicon chips' are assemblages of quantities of these elements and others on single slices of semi-conducting material, but even the mention of a transistor will strike terror into the heart of some of the most electrically competent railway modellers.

Why, then, should the average railway modeller get to grips with electronics? The answer is that the semi-conductor revolution that has taken place since the 1939-45 war has been of immense practical value to the hobby. Transistors might have been invented with model railways especially in mind, since they operate in the same ranges of voltage and current and, moreover, they are very small, inexpensive and reliable. Many railway modellers enjoy the use of transistorised controllers, which offer much finer control of speed—especially in starting, stopping and low-speed running—than is possible with conventional designs. Light-emitting diodes offer a diminutive and long-lived source of coloured light which have almost limitless applications in railway modelling.

Electronic logic circuits make it possible for trains to operate signals or turnouts (points) automatically and even to send commands to their own controllers providing, for example, automatic prototypically smooth station stops. Recently introduced track circuit units provide for the electronic detection of trains on a stretch of track without any modification of track or trains.

The 'silicon chip' has already made inroads into the hobby. A sophisticated controller circuit can be miniaturised to such a degree that it can be installed on board a locomotive, which then runs on permanently live track, the controller chip responding to encoded instructions generated in a master control unit, which may incorporate a microprocessor (miniature computer). In this way a number of trains and accessories can be controlled independently on the same layout using only a two-wire connection between control unit and track. Several such systems are on the market. 'Chip' technology is also facilitating on-board locomotive sound simulation, programmed to respond to the controller setting.

This book attempts to break new ground: as it is intended for railway modellers, readers are assumed to be familiar with volts, switches and short circuits, but no previous knowledge of electronic devices is needed. The main body of the book is a series of 31 projects for electronic circuits for use in connection with model railways. Any railway modeller ought to be able to construct any of these circuits without difficulty, but those with no previous knowledge of electronics are advised first to *read* Projects 1 to 5, which introduce the components which are the building bricks of electronic circuits, and then—referring as necessary to the practical appendices—to *construct* Projects 1 to 5 as a practical exercise. Even if these are not wanted on the layout, they will give the average enthusiast a lot of fun, a basic insight into electronics and the confidence to proceed with more advanced projects.

Readers who want to obtain a deeper understanding of the theory underlying electronic circuits will find this in the theory appendices at the end of the book. These are given for reference only; there is no need for the 'purely practical man' to turn to them unless he wants to, but it has been the present author's experience that a sound knowledge of the theory is indispensable when confronted with a problem in the design or repair of an electronic circuit. The reader who masters the content of this book should be able to initiate his own designs and to progress to more complex projects, such as those using integrated circuits, which have been left out of this book.

Integrated circuits ('chips') have been deliberately omitted from the projects in this book for two reasons. Firstly in five years of model railway electronics experience the author has never found a 'chip' that is useful in the field. Secondly 'chips' are of necessity complex devices and the aim of this book has been to keep the projects as simple as possible for the benefit of new-comers to electronics.

Finally, a word of warning to those who, like the author, are born dabblers! This book is intended to show how electronics can be the means to a more interesting and more realistic model railway, although electronics is a thoroughly absorbing subject in its own right and is followed by many hobbyists as an end in itself. It is also extremely versatile. The author therefore accepts no responsibility for diverting the railway modellers away from strictly railway-oriented electronic projects into burglar alarms, metal detectors, radio receivers, hi-fi equipment and a whole host of other domestic gadgets, leaving less time for model railways!

Roger S. Amos

Rugby 1980

Part 1

Introductory projects

Preamble

The first five projects in this book have been especially chosen to serve as a practical introduction to electronics for readers who have no previous knowledge of the subject. Nevertheless, experienced readers may also find them useful. Projects 1 to 3 involve a natural progression. Project 1—a protection circuit for sidings—must represent the simplest possible electronic circuit since it consists simply of one silicon diode. Not only does this simplest-of-all circuit provide the railway modeller with a useful security system, but it also introduces him to the high-technology world of the semi-conductor. Project 2 is an add-on unit for Project 1, an indicator using a light-emitting diode (LED). Lighting up when the train has arrived, this is useful when the siding is out of sight of the operator. It also introduces the LED, another kind of semi-conductor diode of immense practical value to the railway modeller, and the resistor, one of the 'nuts and bolts' of electronics. Project 3 improves the realism of the siding protection circuit by facilitating a gentle slow-down rather than a sudden stop, and it introduces the reader to the capacitor, another of those 'nuts and bolts'.

Project 4 takes off at a tangent. It is a very simple colour-light signalling system requiring no modification to locomotives and often none to the track. It introduces the reed relay, not strictly an electronic device, but a useful component, nevertheless. This project serves to consolidate what was learned in the earlier projects and shows how remarkable sophistication can be achieved even without transistors. Lastly, Project 5 improves the performance of Project 4 by introducing a transistor.

At the end of this sequence of projects the reader will therefore have encountered resistors, capacitors, silicon diodes, LEDs, transistors and reed relays. These comprise 99 per cent of the components used in model railway electronics. The projects describe the circuit, its functioning and application and draw attention to any special features. Step-by-step instructions are *not* given for two reasons. Firstly, the intended readership consists of railway modellers who will be accustomed to assembling projects, albeit not electronic ones. Secondly, instructions are boring and it is futile to say, 'Solder A to B' when it is obvious from the circuit diagram that A must be joined to B and soldering is the accepted means of doing so. Guidance on soldering and methods of construction will be found in the Practical Appendices that make up Part 8 of the book.

Readers with no previous experience of electronics are advised first to *read* through Projects 1 to 5, then Appendices 1 to 3 and then to construct Projects 1 to 5. The reader who successfully manages these may then proceed with confidence to projects in the following parts of this book.

Project 1: Diode protection for sidings

One of the petty irritations in model railway operation is the disruption caused by derailments when a train at speed hits the buffers at the end of a siding—or, worse, runs off the track if the siding is bufferless. This is especially likely to happen if the siding is out of sight of the operator. One way of preventing this sort of accident is to isolate the end of the siding by means of a rail break or an insulating fishplate and to connect the power to the isolated siding end by means of a switch on the control panel. The power is switched off as the train approaches the end of the siding, so the train will stop as soon as the last set of wheels fitted with power pick-ups crosses the rail break. Of course, to get the train out of the siding the switch must be operated to restore the power to the siding end. This demands a switch and a length of twin-flex wire; both are cumbersome and expensive.

The same effect can be achieved automatically and cheaply by replacing the switch with a silicon diode of suitable rating (see Figure 1.1). The train will always stop as soon as the last power pick-up has crossed the rail break but, on turning the controller to reverse, the train will run out again normally. The diode acts as an automatic switch, blocking 'into-siding' current, but allowing 'out-of-siding' current to pass. It is, of course, important to ensure that the diode is connected the right way round. If it is connected the wrong way round, the train will not be stopped as it runs down the siding and turning the controller to reverse will fail to bring it back. If this happens, take the diode out, turn it round and put it back into the circuit.

How it works

It is a gross oversimplification to say that the diode conducts electricity in one direction only, but for practical purposes this is near enough to the truth. The diode has two terminals or leads called the *anode* and the *cathode*; the cathode is usually marked by a spot or a band on the body of the device; alternatively the cathode end may have a wide 'lip' to it. Inside the device is a tiny piece of silicon which has been 'doped' with two different impurities to give it a negatively charged n-zone (the cathode) and a positively charged p-zone (the anode); the interface between these zones is called the *junction*. Electrons, which are the 'carriers' of electric current, find it easier to pass from the n-zone to the p-zone than in the opposite direction. So, when the anode is connected to a higher voltage (ie, a voltage more *positive*) than that on the cathode, the diode will conduct current quite freely; under these conditions it is said to be *forward biased*. But when the anode is at a lower voltage (ie, less positive or more negative) than that on the cathode, the diode blocks current; only a negligible leakage current passes. The diode is now said to be *reverse biased*. However, if the reverse voltage is great enough, the junction 'breaks down' and reverse current will flow freely.

Choosing the right diode for the job

It is essential to chose a diode whose 'peak inverse voltage' (PIV) rating is high enough for the application. For this project a minimum PIV of 50 V (volts) is sufficient. Too low a PIV could mean that under certain conditions junction breakdown would occur, causing malfunction of the circuit. Also the current that can pass through a diode is limited by the area of the junction; too high a current will cause it to overheat. It is therefore also essential to choose a device capable of handling the current which it will encounter in its application. In this project the minimum current rating permissible is 1 A (Amp). Any of the 1N4001 series of rectifier diodes would be suitable.

Figure 1.2 relates the internal structure of a silicon diode to its external appearance and also gives the symbols used in circuit diagrams.

Parts required

1 silicon diode, 50 PIV, 1 A minimum, eg, any of the 1N4000 series.

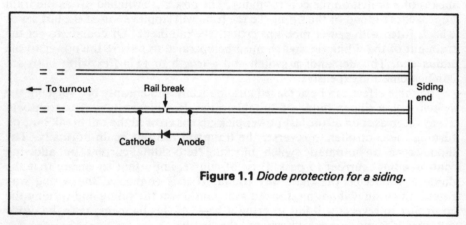

Figure 1.1 *Diode protection for a siding.*

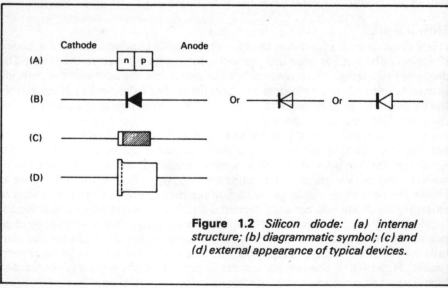

Figure 1.2 *Silicon diode: (a) internal structure; (b) diagrammatic symbol; (c) and (d) external appearance of typical devices.*

Project 2: LED indicator for protected siding

If the diode-protected siding in Project 1 is out of sight of the operator, he will have no way of knowing when the train has arrived and been stopped at the end of the siding. It is, however, easy to arrange for a simple visual indication to be given using a light-emitting diode (LED).

Light-emitting diodes (LEDs)

LEDs are invaluable to railway modellers as miniature, long-lived sources of coloured light. In later projects we shall see how they can be used in colour-light signals and as train headlamps and tail lamps. Their simplest use, however, is as indicators. The diode used in Project 1 was a silicon diode; LEDs resemble silicon diodes in some respects, but the semi-conducting material from which they are constructed is an alloy of gallium, phosphorus and arsenic, the proportions of which determine the colour of light emitted. Like silicon diodes they conduct electricity one way only, and of course, it is when conducting electricity that they emit light. The circuit diagram symbol (Figure 2.1a) is as for a silicon diode, but the parallel arrows suggest light being emitted. They are, however, highly susceptible to damage by reverse voltages (as low as 3 V) and by overheating. Extreme care must be taken in the design of the circuits using LEDs to preclude the possibility of reverse voltages; care must also be taken when soldering connections to LEDs to avoid overheating them and to ensure that the LED is being connected the right way round. Often the cathode is adjacent to a notch in the body of the device (Figure 2.1b), but it is best to test the device first using a 3 V battery via a 100 Ohm resistor to check which lead is which. When the train has been stopped on the diode-protected siding, the silicon diode is reverse biased and so blocks the current to it. If we now connect the LED so that it is parallel to the first diode, but anode to cathode, the LED will light as soon as the train arrives.

In practice it is not quite so simple. The LED would overheat and burn out at once. For most LEDs the maximum current that can be passed is 30 mA (milliAmps—1 mA = 1/1,000 Amp), cf, the typical current taken by a model locomotive, around 250 mA. So a resistor must be added in series with the LED both to limit the current to a safe level and to ensure that the train is stopped.

Resistors

A *resistor* is an electronic component which allows a specific amount of current to pass; the current is in fact proportional to the voltage applied and the ratio of current to voltage for each resistor is known as its *resistance*. Resistance is measured in Ohms (abbreviated Ω); high resistances are in KilOhms (KΩ or just K—1 K = 1,000 Ω); even higher resistances are in MegOhms (MΩ or just M—1 M = 1,000,000 Ω or 1,000 K). Now 1Ω is the resistance which allows 1 A to pass for each volt applied.

It just happens that the maximum voltage available from most controllers is around 20 V and so the resistance needed for this application is 20 V/20 mA = 1 K. So we need a 1 K resistor to protect the LED. Some resistors are marked with their value in figures, but most use an internationally accepted colour code (see Appendix 4). For those not wishing to memorise the code at this stage 1 K is brown-black-red (starting with the band that is nearest to one end of the device).

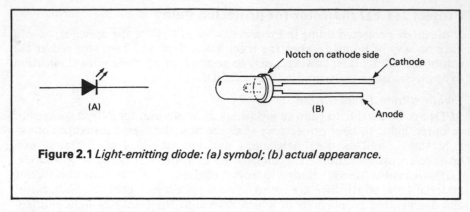

Figure 2.1 *Light-emitting diode: (a) symbol; (b) actual appearance.*

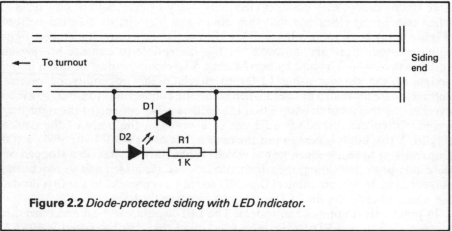

Figure 2.2 *Diode-protected siding with LED indicator.*

Figure 2.2 shows the circuit diagram for the siding protection system with LED indicator. The rectangular symbol is the resistor; this symbol is a new international standard, but many publishers still use an older symbol, which is a zigzag line; readers should recognise this when they see it.

How the circuit works
When the train crosses the rail break silicon diode D1 blocks the heavy current which it needs as before. But LED D2 can conduct current via resistor R1 and the train motor. This current will be limited by the resistor to a maximum of about 20 mA—enough to light the LED brightly, but not enough to keep the train running. As long as the controller is left set 'forwards' (ie, into the siding) the LED will remain lit up, indicating that the train has arrived and been stopped. When the controller is turned to stop or reverse, the LED will be extinguished. On turning the controller to reverse, the train will run out of the siding normally, as before. Incidentally the silicon diode protects the LED against inverse voltages; the forward voltage across D1 (which is also the inverse voltage across D2) cannot exceed around 1 V.

Although the circuit diagram in Figure 2.2 suggests that the LED is physically adjacent to silicon diode D1, this need not necessarily be so. If the siding is out of sight of the operator, the LED may be mounted on a control panel or mimic diagram to give the operator immediate indication of the arrival of the unseen train. This may, of course, necessitate the use of long leads under the baseboard.

Parts required
As Project 1, plus the following:
1 light-emitting diode, size, shape and colour to choice of operator.
1 1 K resistor ½ Watt.
Twin-flex connecting wire (if necessary).

Project 3: Diode-protected siding with gradual slow-down

Useful though it is, the diode protection system in Projects 1 and 2 is very unrealistic in its operation. A locomotive approaching the end of the siding has its power cut off dead as its final power-pick-up wheels cross the rail break, causing an abrupt stop that is far from prototypical. A gentler and more realistic slow-down can be achieved by introducing a capacitor into the circuit.

Capacitors

A *capacitor*, as its name suggests, has an electrical *capacity*—it can store electricity. The earliest capacitors consisted of two metal plates separated by an insulator, which was often an air gap. This construction is suggested by the diagrammatic symbol shown in Figure 3.1a. If the two plates are connected to the terminals of a battery, current will flow while an electrostatic charge builds up between the plates. But as the charge builds up the current falls and, after a certain time, when the capacitor is fully charged, the current stops altogether. The capacitor may now be disconnected from the battery and yet retain its charge. It may be connected to a suitable circuit, when it will *discharge*—the same electricity that charged it up now leaves the capacitor as a discharge current. This current gradually diminishes until the capacitor is fully discharged.

The unit of electrical capacitance is the Farad (F), but the Farad itself is a massive unit not normally encountered in electronics. In model railway electronics most of the capacitors have capacitances in microfarads (μF); (1,000,000 μF = 1 F). Many high-value capacitors are formed by a chemical process and are known as *electrolytic capacitors*. Unlike most other sorts of capacitor these are *polarised*, ie, the terminals are labelled positive and negative and for correct operation the component must be connected the right way round; the terminal labelled positive must be kept positive (or neutral) relative to the other terminal. Polarised capacitors are distinguished in circuit diagrams by the symbol shown in Figure 3.1b; the 'hollow' side is always positive.

Another feature to watch for in capacitors is the maximum working voltage. This is given on the side of the device and must not be exceeded or damage may result.

How the circuit works

Figure 3.2 shows the diode-protection circuit of Project 2 (including LED indicator) rearranged somewhat to incorporate a slow-down capacitor. This is

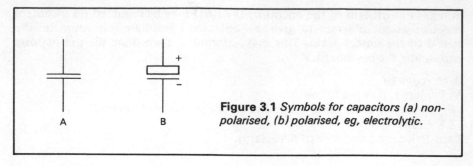

Figure 3.1 *Symbols for capacitors (a) non-polarised, (b) polarised, eg, electrolytic.*

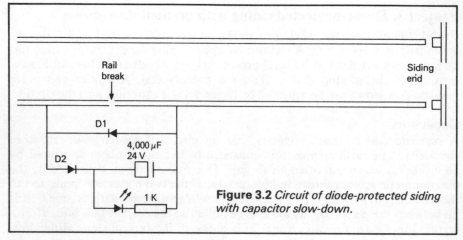

Figure 3.2 *Circuit of diode-protected siding with capacitor slow-down.*

a 4,000 μF electrolytic type and in the author's prototype was rated for 40 V. The capacitor is added in parallel with the original silicon diode and a second silicon diode (of the same rating as the first) is added in series with the capacitor. This is essential—it prevents the capacitor from being discharged and recharged the wrong way round when the controller is set to reverse. Note that the LED indicator and its current-limiting resistor are now connected across the terminals of the capacitor.

When the locomotive crosses the rail break, diode D1 blocks its current as before, but now there is an alternative route by which power can still reach the locomotive; this is via the capacitor. However, as it charges up, this current diminishes. So the locomotive slows down gently as the capacitor charges and comes to a standstill as the capacitor becomes fully charged. The LED lights up as the capacitor charges and if power is left on 'forwards' (ie, into the siding) the locomotive will remain stationary and the LED will remain lit up, as before.

The LED will remain lit up for a while even after the controller has been turned to stop or to reverse. When either of these happen the capacitor begins to discharge, its only discharge route being via the LED; D2 is now reverse biased. So for as long as the capacitor takes to discharge (20 seconds or so) the LED will remain lit up, but gradually fading. It is a good idea to include the LED indicator in this circuit for two reasons. One is that it provides a discharge path for the capacitor, which would otherwise retain its charge for minutes or even hours. The other is that it serves to show when the capacitor is discharged. When the LED goes out, discharge is complete and the circuit is now ready to slow down another train gently. When the controller is turned to reverse, the locomotive will run out normally as in Projects 1 and 2. D2 remains reverse biased so that the discharge of the capacitor is not affected by the locomotive movement.

Practical considerations
The capacitor is a bulky object and will probably need to be concealed under the baseboard. Otherwise the circuit should present no special difficulties.

Parts required
2 silicon diodes, 50 PIV, 1 A minimum, eg, 1N4000 series.
1 electrolytic capacitor, 4,000 μF, 24 V working minimum.
1 light emitting diode, size and colour to choice of operator.
1 1K resistor, $\frac{1}{2}$ W (brown/black/red).

Project 4: Simple automatic colour-light signalling system
In Projects 2 and 3 a very simple electronic circuit caused an LED to light up when a train arrived on a certain stretch of track, namely the diode-protected end of a siding. This led the author to think that with a little ingenuity it ought to be possible for a train to change a colour-light signal automatically. The system described in this project is crude, but simple and the signal itself can be used with the more sophisticated control circuits described in Part 5.

The model signal
The signal lamps are two LEDs, one red and one green, connected in parallel, cathode to anode, as shown in Figure 4.1. Using this arrangement each LED protects the other against inverse voltages and the signal requires only a two-wire connection. The polarity of the supply determines which LED lights. If A is more positive than B, the red LED lights; and if B is more positive than A, the green LED lights. But if A and B are at about the same voltage, no current will flow, so neither will light. Construction of the signal itself is a scenic matter and strictly beyond the scope of this book, but because the leads of the LEDs were put to scenic use on the author's 4 mm scale signals, his technique is illustrated in Figure 4.2.

The control circuit
Put crudely the signal is electrically 'strung' between the output of the controller and a 9 V battery. When the voltage from the controller is higher than that from the battery, the green LED lights up. When the voltage from the controller is lower than that from the battery, the red LED lights up. When a train is running in the section, guarded by the signal, the input from the controller is short-circuited, bringing the red LED on.

There are two problems to overcome. One is that the voltage from the controller can be of either polarity, depending on whether it is set to 'forwards' or 'reverse'. To prevent this from upsetting the comparison a *bridge rectifier circuit* is inserted between the controller and the signal. A

bridge rectifier is a rather cunning arrangement of four diodes shown in Figure
4.3. These diodes marshal the input current in such a way that, no matter what
the polarity of the input is, the output polarity is always the same: work it out
for yourself if you like. The second problem is that most controllers deliver a
pulsed output, not a steady one. Between the pulses the battery would always
'win' so that even with the controller on full power the two LEDs would flash
alternately and both would appear to be 'on' together. So a capacitor is added
across the output of the bridge rectifier. This charges up during the pulses and
retains most of the controller output voltage between the pulses.

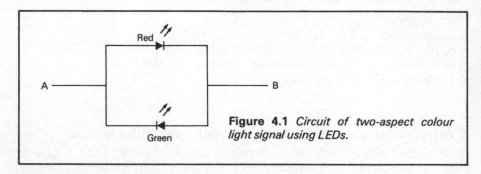

Figure 4.1 *Circuit of two-aspect colour light signal using LEDs.*

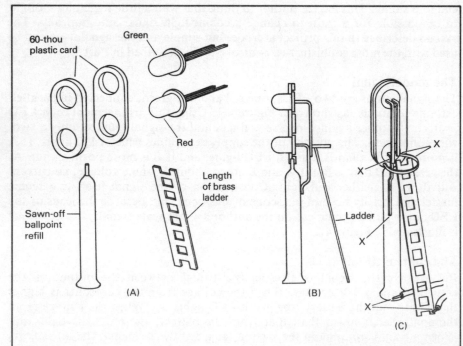

Figure 4.2 *One method of constructing a two-aspect LED signal: (a) exploded view; (b) cross section; (c) rear view of completed signal. X marks each soldered joint.*

Figure 4.4 shows the circuit so far. The additional diode D5 is to prevent the controller from 'recharging' the battery. If this is attempted with dry batteries they are liable to explode, which is most unpleasant, if not downright dangerous. Any small-signal silicon diode (eg, 1N914) can be used for D5. Resistors R1 and R2 are necessary to complete the circuit; without them D3 and D4 would be in opposition to D5 and no current could flow at all. R3 helps to get the changeover level right.

To feed information about the presence of a train in the section being guarded into the circuit we need to isolate electrically the section of track (in one rail only) and to monitor the current being fed from the controller to that section. If your layout is already divided into sections for 'cab control' and you are willing to make your control sections serve also as signalling sections, this job is done for you. The current is monitored by passing it through the coil of a reed relay.

Reed relays

A *reed switch* consists of a pair of gold-plated soft-iron contacts in a vacuum in a glass envelope (see Figure 4.5a). Normally the contacts are apart, so the switch is 'off'. In the presence of a suitable magnetic field, however, the contacts become mutually attracted and they close. This magnetic field may be provided by a permanent magnet; a traditional method of train detection (Project 15) is to fit reed switches to the track to be operated by magnets fixed beneath the trains. Alternatively the magnetic field may be provided by an electromagnet, ie, a coil though which an electric current is passing. Ideally this coil surrounds the reed switch itself. This reed switch/coil combination is known as a *reed relay*. Figure 4.5b gives the symbol for a reed switch used in circuit diagrams and Figure 4.5c gives that for a coil; when the two are in close proximity, suggesting a connection, the symbols together represent a reed relay.

A suitable relay for this project can be made up in a few minutes by even the most ham-fisted by simply winding a coil around the body of a reed switch. Copper coil wire—the scanning coils from discarded TV picture tubes or unwanted transformers or motors are useful sources—should be used. The number of turns needed will depend on the characteristics of the reed switch you are using and is best found by trial and error, but the author found that, with miniature reed switches from Tandy, 50 turns gave a threshold current (ie, the minimum coil current that will turn the switch on) of about 40 mA, a suitable level.

The feed from the controller to the track section being signalled is passed through the coil of the reed relay. If there is a train (or a short circuit) in the section and the controller is delivering power, the reed switch contacts will close. If the controller delivers pulses, the contacts will close at the onset of each pulse and open at the end of each, making a just audible 'ringing' sound.

The reed switch itself is connected in parallel with the capacitor in the control circuit. So, if current is being consumed in the section (suggesting the presence of a train), the voltage from the controller is short circuited and the signal goes to red. The complete circuit is shown in Figure 4.6. An extra resistor R3 must be added to the circuit. This has two purposes. If the controller delivers pulses it is important that the charge on the capacitor be kept low when there is a train running in the section; R3 restricts the rate at

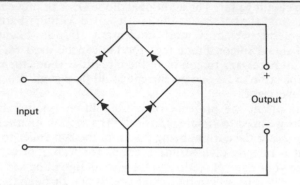

Figure 4.3 *Bridge rectifier circuit.*

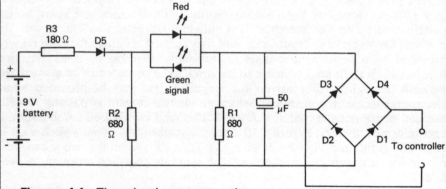

Figure 4.4 *The signal compares the controller output voltage with that of the battery.*

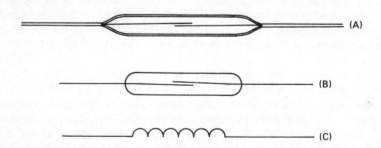

Figure 4.5 *Reed switches and relays: (a) appearance of typical reed switch; (b) graphic symbol for a reed switch; (c) symbol for a coil. The juxtaposition of (b) and (c) represents a reed relay.*

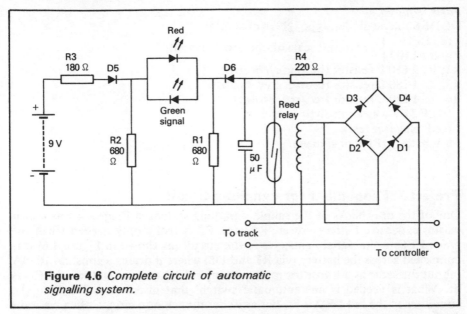

Figure 4.6 *Complete circuit of automatic signalling system.*

which the capacitor can recharge. (The switch contacts do not necessarily close for the entire duration of the pulses and without this resistor the charge could rise rapidly enough to bring on the green light.) Secondly the resistor protects the reed switch contacts which would otherwise be directly across the output of the bridge rectifier, ie, directly across the output of the controller. An excessive current would pass on closure of the contacts, which could cause the melting or even vaporisation of the gold plating, rendering the switch useless; learn from the author's mistakes—he has seen it happen! The extra diode D6 prevents the red LED from taking excessive current when the reed switch contacts close.

For its simplicity the circuit works remarkably well; the author's prototype captivated all who saw it working, model railway enthusiasts or not. The signal will be green when a train is 'expected' in the section, ie, the section is empty and power is applied. As soon as the train passes the signal and enters the section, the light changes to red and remains red as long as the train is in the section. Even if the train is stopped and the controller plug is pulled out, the signal remains correctly at red. When power is restored and the train leaves the section, the signal correctly turns back to green automatically.

The circuit has three failings. Firstly, despite appearances true automatic signalling logic is not conserved. When the section is vacant but there is no power from the controller, the signal shows red, drawing power from the battery (remember to disconnect the battery when the system is not in use). Secondly, at certain low settings of the controller (which are generally passed through rapidly in stopping and starting) the signal is extinguished momentarily. The purist wanting a closer approach to prototypical signalling must turn to train detection systems such as those described in Part 5 to give a true indication of the presence of trains in sections. Thirdly, the circuit wastes expensive power from the battery through R1. This waste at least can be eliminated, as will be seen in Project 5.

Parts required
D1-D6 6 silicon diodes, type 1N914 or similar.
1 red LED }
1 green LED } size to suit scale of operator's layout.
R1, R2 2 680 Ω resistor (blue/grey/brown).
R3   1 180 Ω resistor (brown/grey/brown).
R4   1 220 Ω resistor (red/red/brown).
1 50 μF 24 V wkg electrolytic capacitor.
1 reed relay (see text).
1 9 V battery (PP 9 or similar).

Project 5: Economiser for signalling circuit

One of the drawbacks of the simple signalling system in Project 4 was that it wastes expensive battery power. Resistor R2 is really only needed when the *green* LED in the signal lights, yet in the circuit (as shown in Figure 4.6) it is connected across the battery (via R3 and D5) where it drains a constant 10 mA (about the same as a transistor radio playing softly) even when the red LED is lit. What is needed is an 'automatic switch' that disconnects R2 from the circuit when the red LED is lit, but switches it back into circuit when we want the green LED to light. We could use another reed relay as an 'automatic switch', but a reed relay is comparatively costly and its coil would consume more current than we should be saving. Fortunately there is a device that is inexpensive and in this application would consume practically no extra current—this is the transistor.

Transistors

We made the acquaintance of silicon diodes in Projects 1 to 4. Transistors allow for even more precise control of electric current. Whereas a diode has only two terminals, a transistor has three; they are called the *collector*, the *emitter* and the *base*. The current flowing between the collector and the emitter (called the *collector current*) is controlled by the current flowing between the base and the emitter (called the *base bias*). When there is no base bias, there will be no collector current, except for a negligible leakage current. The base bias is generally much smaller than the collector current which it controls— under ideal conditions the collector current may be as much as 500 times as great as the base current controlling it, but conditions are rarely ideal and 100 is a more typical figure. This figure, the current gain or α, varies widely with conditions, with the transistor type used and even between individual transistors of the same nominal type.

The transistor for our project is an npn general-purpose type, such as a BC 108 or 2N2222. In an npn transistor both the collector and the base need to be kept positive relative to the emitter. (There are also, however, pnp transistors whose collector and base must be negative relative to the emitter.) Figure 5.1 shows the circuit diagram symbols for npn and pnp transistors. Note that the emitter is distinguished from the collector by an arrow and that the direction of the arrow indicates whether the transistor is an npn or pnp type. The arrow (like the arrow in the diode symbol, forward bias assumed) points towards the negative terminal of the power supply or battery.

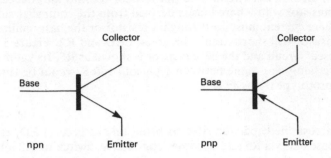

Figure 5.1 *Graphic symbols for npn and pnp transistors.*

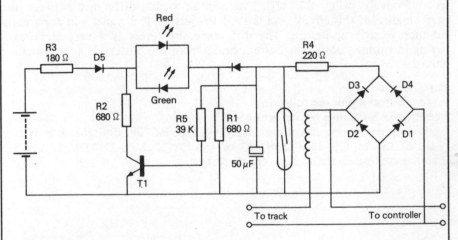

Figure 5.2 *Circuit of the signalling system with the transistor economiser.*

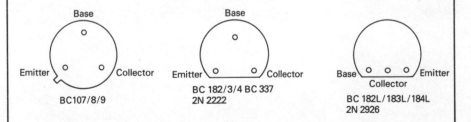

Figure 5.3 *Lead configurations of some suitable transistors — bottom views.*

All that is needed, then, in our circuit is to put resistor R2 into the collector circuit of an npn transistor whose base bias is derived from the controller side of the circuit. The base current must go through a resistor or the base/emitter junction of the transistor will short-circuit the green LED and R2. Figure 5.2 shows the 'economised' circuit and the base resistor is shown as R5. Its value is uncritical; almost certainly any value between 10 K and 100 K would be fine; but in the author's prototype it was 39 K.

How it works

When the voltage across the capacitor rises to bring on the green LED, the transistor receives base bias via R5 and becomes conductive, switching R2 into the circuit. Current from the controller now flows via the transistor, R2 and the green LED, which of course lights up. However, when the voltage across the capacitor is very low (either because there is no output from the controller or because the reed relay contacts are permanently or intermittently closed by a train running in the section), there will be no base current and the transistor will effectively switch R2 'off'. There is no visible difference between the performance of this circuit and that of Project 4. The signal will apparently function exactly as before. The difference, however, is a very significant saving in running costs; the current drain from the battery is approximately halved.

Parts needed

As for Project 4 plus the following:

1 resistor 39 K (orange/white/orange).

1 general purpose npn silicon transistor, eg, type BC108. (Suitable alternatives are BC107 or 109, BC182 or 183 or 184, 2N2222 or 2N2926. Figure 5.3 shows the lead configurations for these.)

Part 2

Controllers

Preamble

The purpose of a controller is, of course, to regulate the direction and speed of a model train. An ideal controller would give infinitely variable control of speed from a barely perceptible crawl—a scale 1 mph, say—to full speed, which may be a scale 100 mph or more for a modern express passenger train. Moreover it should give prototypically smooth starts and stops.

Until the advent of transistorised circuits, controllers were of two types. Commonest was the *rheostat* type in which a heavy-duty rheostat (variable resistor) in series with the locomotive motor provided some control of current and therefore of speed. Rheostat controllers have either a simple rheostat with a separate changeover switch for direction or a split-track rheostat, direction control being combined with the speed control, which has a central 'stop' position. The latter is more complex and expensive, but easier to use and more reliable. Switches are a frequent cause of faults in controllers and their use is best avoided wherever possible.

The other type of controller uses a *variable transformer*, in which the magnetic coupling between primary and secondary windings is adjustable, providing a means of varying the output voltage and therefore the speed. Both types of controller are still made and widely used. The controllers provided by the ready-to-run model railway manufacturers are generally rheostat types.

However both types of controller pose problems with which the reader will probably be only too familiar. Imagine your train standing in the station ready to leave. You advance the speed control and nothing happens. You advance it further and still nothing happens. You advance it to perhaps 75 per cent of full power when suddenly the train bolts from the station with the abruptness of a bullet leaving a gun! You can now turn the speed control down to 25 per cent, say, of full power and reduce the train's speed to a reasonable level but it is too late; the illusion has been destroyed. Prototype trains—even electric types with brisk acceleration—pull away smoothly and take appreciable time to accelerate to normal cruising speed, an effect which it is often difficult to reproduce in miniature using a conventional controller.

The reason for this lies in the characteristics of model locomotives and of conventional controllers. A stationary train—even if it consists only of a 'light' locomotive—has considerable inertia. To overcome this and set the train rolling demands considerable power and therefore a high current. This is why the train will not begin to move until the speed control is well advanced.

As soon as the inertia has been overcome, and the train has begun to roll, rather less power is needed to keep it moving. So unless the speed control is turned down as soon as the train begins to move—and there is no practicable way of knowing exactly when to turn it down and how far—the train will race away in a thoroughly unprototypical manner.

Model railway manufacturers have attempted to tackle this problem from the motor end rather than the controller end. Permanent-magnet motors have gentler characteristics if the armature windings are small relative to the size of the magnets. So either a conventional small magnet is used with an armature having five, or even seven, small poles or a conventional three-pole armature is completely enclosed between a pair of massive permanent magnets; the latter is known as a ring-field motor. Even with these, however, it can be difficult to achieve realistic smooth starts with a conventional controller.

Transistors, as we saw in Project 5, provide precise control of electric currents and transistor technology has made possible great advances in electric motor control. There are two principal techniques employed in electronic controllers. One is *closed-loop* operation in which the controller itself monitors the conditions prevailing in the motor and adjusts its output as appropriate; this is rather like having an 'automatic hand' to turn down the speed control at just the right moment to prevent the train racing away on starting. The other technique is *pulse-width modulation* (PWM); a PWM controller delivers not a steady current, but a series of pulses of full power, speed being regulated by varying the length (or 'width') of the pulses. In practice many electronic controllers employ elements of both techniques. Projects 6 to 8 describe closed-loop controllers of increasing sophistication. Projects 9 and 10 are concerned with PWM circuits.

Project 6: Simple closed-loop controller

In a closed-loop controller the voltage across the motor, ie, that at the output of the controller, is compared with a control voltage set by the speed control. The voltage across the motor will consist not only of that coming from the controller, but also a component coming from the motor itself, which acts as a generator when its armature turns—this is called the 'back EMF'. Other conditions being equal, the back EMF is proportional to motor speed and inversely proportional to the work being done by the motor. By comparing this voltage with that set on the speed control a closed-loop controller compensates for changes in gradient or loading and prevents sudden unintended surges of speed.

In Project 5 we saw that the collector current of a transistor is controlled by the generally much smaller base bias, both currents emerging on the emitter. If this combined current is used as the base bias for a second transistor, the resulting pair of transistors will give a very high current gain. Known as a *Darlington pair*, this circuit and its variants are widely used in electronics; the basic circuit is shown in Figure 6.1. A simple but effective closed-loop controller can be made using a Darlington pair whose input is derived from a *potentiometer* across the supply and whose output is taken from the emitter of T2. Figure 6.2 shows the practical circuit for this controller.

Potentiometers

Potentiometers are among the most familiar of electronic components, since they form the volume, tone, brightness and contrast controls in domestic audio, radio and TV equipment. A potentiometer consists of a circular (or sometimes straight) carbon track having a specified resistance. It has three terminals: one at each end of the track and a third making electrical contact with a slider which can be moved by means of the control knob to contact any point along the length of the carbon track. Figure 6.3 shows the construction and external appearance of a typical rotary potentiometer.

Its circuit diagram symbol and mode of operation is shown in Figure 6.4. As the symbol suggests, it may be thought of as a resistor with an adjustable tapping. In the circuit of Figure 6.4, when the slider is at the top of the track, the output voltage will equal the input voltage. When the slider is at the bottom of the track, the output voltage will be zero, ie, equal to the 'ground' or 'earth' side of the circuit, to which it is now short-circuited. When the slider is at an intermediate position between the ends of the track, an intermediate output voltage will be obtained; any output voltage between zero and the input voltage can be obtained by moving the slider to the appropriate point.

Potentiometers are available with track resistances ranging from 1 K to 1 M and following linear (resistance proportional to distance on track) or logarithmic (resistance proportional to logarithm of distance on track) laws. They resemble rheostats but are in generally higher resistance ranges and are cheaper and more compact, providing a second advantage of electronic controllers over rheostat types.

How the controller works

The circuit as shown in Figure 6.2 must be connected to a suitable power supply, which we will consider in more detail later on. The potentiometer P1 is, of course, the speed control and is used as a source of base bias (via the current-limiting resistor R1) for the Darlington pair T1/T2. We saw in Project 5 that in an npn transistor the base voltage must be positive relative to the emitter if conduction is to occur. This is because the transistor contains (between its base and emitter terminals) a pn junction resembling that in a diode; in an npn transistor the base behaves as the anode. While this junction is forward biased, base bias will flow stimulating collector current, but if the base/emitter junction is reverse biased, base bias is blocked and so collector current will also stop.

Now apply this to the circuit of our controller. As long as the voltage on the base of T1 is healthily positive relative to the voltage on the emitter of T2, which is the voltage across our locomotive motor, the transistors will conduct and supply current to the track. However, if the voltage across the motor rises, eg, if the motor begins racing and develops extra back EMF, so that the voltage on the emitter of T2 approaches that on the base of T1, the current being delivered to the track will be reduced and may even be cut off altogether, slowing the train and compensating for the burst of speed.

The controller is therefore what electronics buffs would call a 'voltage follower'. The output voltage follows the input voltage, ie, that set by the potentiometer. In practice it is generally about 1.4 V lower; there is a loss of about 0.7 V across a forward-biased silicon junction. We shall meet this 'diode drop' again and again. By adjusting the speed control any output voltage

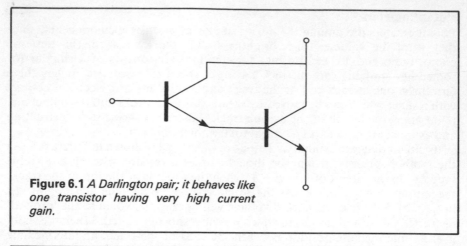

Figure 6.1 *A Darlington pair; it behaves like one transistor having very high current gain.*

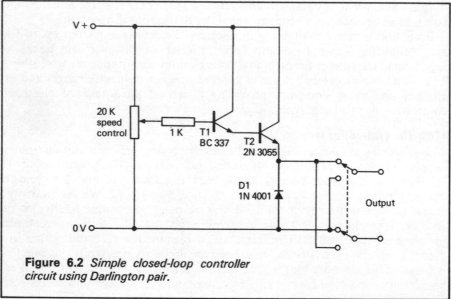

Figure 6.2 *Simple closed-loop controller circuit using Darlington pair.*

between zero and the supply voltage (less 1.4 V) can be obtained and the motor is free to draw as much current as it likes at any voltage—provided certain limits (such as automatic cut-out thresholds) are not exceeded.

Diode D1 protects the circuit from the effects of 'inductive overshoot'. This is a pulse of power generated by a motor just after its external power supply is turned off. When a motor forms the emitter load of a transistor, inductive overshoot can bias the transistor forward even when the speed control is at zero; this has sometimes caused acute embarrassment to experimenters who suddenly find that for some seemingly unaccountable reason they cannot stop their trains! The diode, which under normal circumstances is reverse biased and therefore has no effect on the circuit, harmlessly short-circuits inductive overshoot so that it cannot interfere with the operation of the transistors.

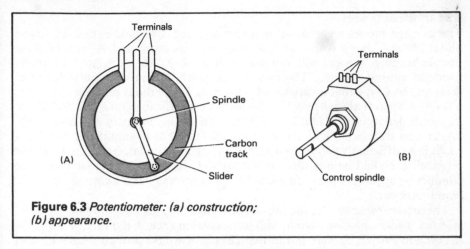

Figure 6.3 *Potentiometer: (a) construction; (b) appearance.*

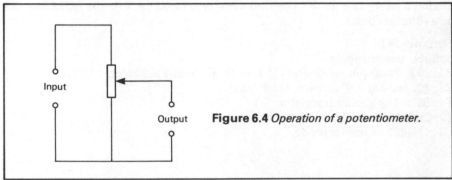

Figure 6.4 *Operation of a potentiometer.*

Circuits like this one are used in some practical controllers and will in general give better results than conventional types. But there are a number of disadvantages. One that we have already noted is that the maximum output voltage is 1.4 V less than the supply voltage. Another disadvantage is that the 'controllability' at low speeds, eg, on starting, is poor. This is because at low speeds the motor back EMF is very small and this circuit is simply not sufficiently sensitive to detect it and make use of it for auto-regulation.

Power supply

Beginners to electronics should not construct mains supply units; these can be purchased quite cheaply ready made. With a 12 V to 16 V smoothed supply there will be ample power, but poor control at low speeds for the reason given above. Better low-speed control will be obtained if an unsmoothed supply is used, but a higher voltage (16 V to 20 V) will be needed for full power.

A controller (or its power supply) *must* incorporate some kind of overload cut-out mechanism to protect its own circuitry, also the transformer and the locomotive from damage by overheating in the event of a short circuit or jammed mechanism. This could be a thermal device incorporated in the power supply unit or an electronic circuit—suitable electronic circuits are described in Part 3.

The transistors used

The average model locomotive at medium speed and moderate load draws about 250 mA, but a worn-out loco may draw as much as 1 A; two of these double-heading a train will obviously draw 2 A, the threshold of many overload cut-out systems. The *output transistor* (T2) in our controller must therefore be a type that is capable of delivering 2 A without burning out. Since a safety margin is always sensible, the ideal device for this job is the 2N3055 or its plastic derivatives (MJ3055, MJE3055); this is the 'industry standard' high-power npn transistor, well known to students of hi-fi amplifiers; rated for 15 A, it is sufficiently robust to withstand rough treatment, both electrical and physical. It should be mounted on a *heat sink*, ie, a block of finned metal to conduct away excess heat. *In closed-loop controllers the output transistors tend to run hot.*

The *driver transistor*, ie, the pre-output stage (T1) also needs to be carefully selected, as its collector current may on occasion exceed 100 mA; if a BC108 (as used in Project 5) were put in this circuit, it would probably have a short life but a merry one. In this position use a type rated for 1 A; the BC337 would be a suitable choice.

Parts needed

Suitable power supply.
P1: 20 K linear potentiometer (25 K or 50 K equally suitable).
R1: 1 K resistor $\frac{1}{2}$ W (brown/black/red).
T1: BC337 or similar transistor.
T2: 2N3055 or similar transistor.
D1: 1N4001 or similar diode.

Project 7: Sensitive closed-loop controller

The simple closed-loop controller in Project 6 gave poor control at very low speeds because it did not have enough gain to detect the infinitesimal back EMF generated by locomotive motors as they begin to turn. The circuit shown in Figure 7.1, however, has an extra transistor giving it enough gain to give a starting and crawling performance which the author has found quite satisfactory. Indeed it can drive an unloaded Hornby XO4 motor at less than 10 rpm and will give realistic, gentle starts with most model locomotives.

The circuit resembles that of Project 6 except that i) the output is taken from the collectors of the Darlington pair, ii) an extra transistor has been added at the front end and iii) a separate feedback loop via diode D1 has been incorporated. Diode D1 blocks inductive overshoot but conducts back EMF, about two thirds of which is fed back to the emitter of T1, which compares it with the control voltage. The diode also prevents T1 emitter current from bypassing resistor R2 via the lower combined resistances of R4 and the motor.

The transistors used

Note that T2 and T3, although still a Darlington pair as in Project 6, are both pnp types. They will behave very like the pair in Project 6 but, of course, all associated polarities will be reversed. It may seem extravagant if you have already constructed Project 6 to have to get fresh transistors for Project 7, especially as the pnp output transistor is likely to cost more than its npn equivalent, but you will need all four if you wish to proceed to Project 8, which the author recommends. If you really want to be a spendthrift, you can use the npn Darlington pair from Project 6 in this project as T2 and T3 providing that you i) use a pnp type for T1, ii) reverse the connections to the power supply and iii) reverse the direction of D1. If you are constructing Project 7 as specified, T1 can be any small-signal npn type, eg, BC108. A heat sink will be needed for T3; see notes on Project 6.

Power supply
The notes for Project 6 apply equally to this project.

Parts needed
Semi-conductors: T1: BC108 or similar small signal npn transistor.
        T2: BC327 or similar 1A pnp transistor.
        T3: MJE2955 or similar pnp power transistor.
        D1: 1N914 or similar small signal silicon diode.
        Resistors $\frac{1}{4}$ W.
        R1: 1K.
        R2: 470 Ω.
        R3: 1 K.
        R4: 220 Ω.
Others: 20 K linear potentiometer.
    2-pole 2-way switch.
    Suitable power supply.
    Tagboard.

In the reverse-polarity version of this circuit T1 = BC178 or similar, T2 = BC337 or similar, T3 = MJE 3055 or similar.

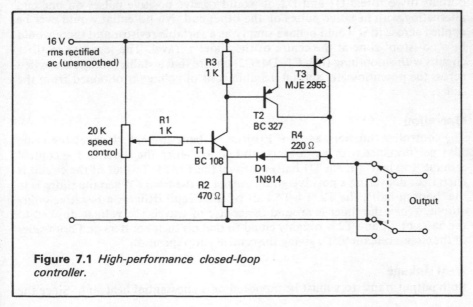

Figure 7.1 *High-performance closed-loop controller.*

Project 8: Bi-directional controller

Both controllers described so far needed a changeover switch for reversing. In the author's experience these are never fully reliable and nothing is more frustrating than a faulty switch in a controller. For ease of operation bi-directional controllers, ie, those in which one knob combines the functions of speed and direction control, cannot be bettered, except, perhaps, by touch control (Project 14). The circuit of Project 7 is eminently suitable for adaption as a bi-directional controller. Comparison of the adapted circuit given in Figure 8.1 with that in Figure 7.1 will show that the new controller is really two controller circuits sharing a common control and a common output circuit. The circuit shows a kind of symmetry, *complementary symmetry*, in which each transistor is 'balanced' by one of the opposite polarity.

Power supply

In this kind of controller there is a danger that both output transistors may—owing to some malfunction—become conductive simultaneously, short circuiting the power supply. With this particular controller, however, this cannot happen because of the unusual power supply. The controller has its own rectifiers and must be connected to an ac supply (preferably 20 V). Separate half-wave unsmoothed rectification is used for each half of the circuit, so the two halves of the circuit are never energised simultaneously. The maximum output voltage as measured on a test meter is only 9 V, but this includes peaks of up to 23 V and even the stickiest locomotives spring to life. Top speed is limited, but quite adequate for normal operations.

Speed control

The unusual rectifier arrangement leads to difficulties with the speed control. The controller depends on a stable control voltage being available at the slider of the potentiometer. If the potentiometer were simply connected between the outputs of rectifiers D1 and D2, it would receive positive pulses on one end alternating with negative pulses on the other end. No potential would ever be applied across it; it would behave simply as a variable resistor and there would be a no 'stop' zone at the centre of the slider's travel. The separate rectifier circuits with smoothing (D3/C1, D4/C2) ensure that a stable voltage is applied across the potentiometer so that a stable control voltage is obtained from the slider.

Operation

The controller functions as two 'Project 7s' back-to-back. It gives the same silky performance with gentle starts and stops. When the slider of the control is in the 'top half' (ie, the D1 half) of travel the T1/T3/T5 half of the circuit is energised, delivering a positive-going output to the track. When the slider is in the 'bottom half', the T2/T4/T6 half of the circuit delivers a negative-going output. When the slider is around the centre of travel, the voltage applied to the bases of T1 and T2 is roughly equal to that on their emitters and both sides of the circuit remain 'off', giving the central 'stop' position.

Heat sinkage

Both output transistors must be mounted on a substantial heat sink. Since the collectors of both are connected, both transistors may be mounted on the same heat sink without any difficulties.

Parts needed

Semi-conductors:	1 × BC108 or similar, 1 × BC178 or similar, 1 × BC337 or similar, 1 × BC327 or similar, 1 × MJE3055 or similar 1 × MJE2955 or similar.
	4 × IN4001 or similar
	4 × IN914.
Resistors:	1 × 220 Ω.
	2 × 470 Ω.
	3 × 1 K.
	1 × 100 K potentiometer.
Capacitors:	2 × 4 µF 40 V electrolytic.
Miscellaneous:	240 V:20 V transformer.
	Thermal overload cut-out.
	Tagboard, heat sink.

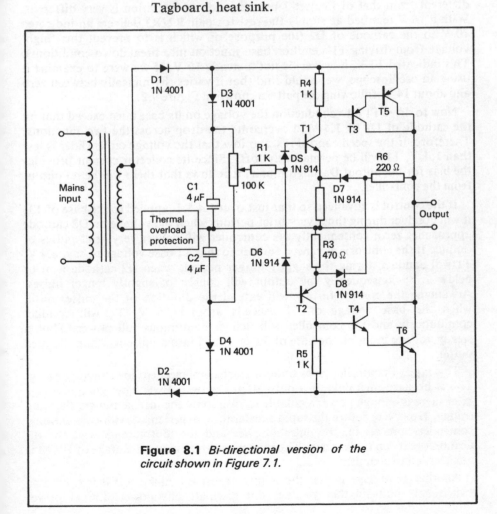

Figure 8.1 *Bi-directional version of the circuit shown in Figure 7.1.*

Project 9: Pulse-width-modulation (PWM) controller

A PWM controller instead of delivering an infinitely variable but more-or-less steady current delivers pulses of *full power*. These pulses are at a frequency that is usually fixed—often at 100 Hz (ie 100 pulses per second) since this can easily be derived from full-wave rectified mains. Speed is controlled by varying the length (or 'width') of the pulses. At low settings of the speed control the pulses are brief compared with the intervals (the 'spaces') between them. As the control is advanced, the pulses become longer and the spaces correspondingly shorter. On some PWM controllers, as the speed control approaches maximum, the pulses merge into each other, the spaces disappearing, so that continuous full power is delivered.

Figure 9.1 gives the circuit of a simple PWM controller. Emitter bias for T1 is derived from unsmoothed full-wave-rectified ac. The rest of the circuit operates from a smoothed supply, diode D1 preventing this smoothing from reaching the bias chain for T1 emitter. Otherwise the circuit is not radically different from that of Project 7 but its mode of operation is very different. With a 16 V rectified ac supply the resistor pair R2/R3 delivers an indicated 10 V to the cathode of D2 (the purpose of which is to prevent this 'high' voltage from driving T1's emitter/base junction into breakdown conditions). This indicated 10 V, however, is not a steady 10 V. If we were to examine it using an oscilloscope, we should find that it varies rhythmically between zero and about 14 V, following the pattern shown in Figure 9.2.

Now to drive T1 into conduction the voltage on its base must exceed that on the cathode of D2 by 1.4 V to overcome the drop across the two junctions. Therefore, if the speed control is set so low that the voltage on its slider is less than 1.4 V, T1 will be permanently 'off'. Since its collector current provides the bias for the output Darlington pair, it follows that there will be no output from the controller.

If the control is advanced so that just over 1.4 V is applied to the base of T1, it will conduct during those very brief periods when the voltage on D2 cathode approaches zero; consequently the controller will deliver very brief pulses of output. If the control is advanced further so that T1 base voltage is, say, 6.4 V, T1 will conduct during the slightly longer periods when D2 cathode is at or below 5 V; consequently the output will consist of slightly longer pulses. Advancing the control further will extend the duration of the pulses until, when the base voltage of T1 exceeds around 16 V, T1 will conduct continuously and the controller will deliver continuous full power. Thus a steady voltage input on the base of T1 is turned into a pulse-width-modulated output.

This type of controller gives smooth starts and excellent low-speed running. This is because each pulse is a pulse of *full power*. Even when the pulses are brief there is enough power available to overcome the inertia and get the train rolling. However, before the rapid acceleration experienced with conventional controllers can set in, the pulse finishes and the motor must wait for the next before it can move again. Thus the most impressive advantage of PWM is its sheer 'controllability'.

Another advantage is that the output transistor runs cool; it is used as a switch only and—in theory—does not dissipate any power. Larger power

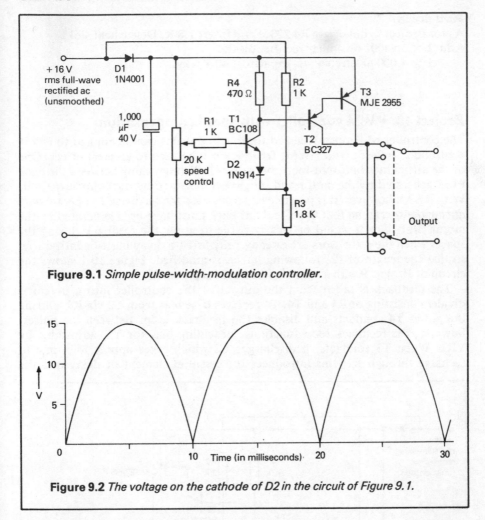

Figure 9.1 *Simple pulse-width-modulation controller.*

Figure 9.2 *The voltage on the cathode of D2 in the circuit of Figure 9.1.*

transistors can be used without heat sinks, but smaller ones are probably best fitted with them.

PWM has its disadvantages. One that will instantly become apparent is noise, especially after the uncanny silence of closed-loop control. PWM makes locos buzz like angry bumble bees. Even this is a disadvantage only with steam-outline locos; with diesels, and especially diesel multiple units, the noise is startlingly realistic. Another disadvantage is motor heating. It is advisable to avoid sustained crawling; at low speeds there is little back EMF to limit the current. Consequently the current passed during the pulses, brief though they are, is high. Once when the author had allowed a Hornby 'Jinty' to crawl with a heavy train for about five minutes, the loco did something alarmingly prototypical—it gave off smoke! Unfortunately this smoke came out of the cab entries, not the chimney. Happily the motor had suffered nothing worse than scorched lacquer on the armature windings, but the incident provided an important lesson about the use of PWM.

Parts needed

As for Project 7, but delete R4 220 Ω and insert 1.8 K. Delete heat sink.
Add: 1 × 1N4001 or similar rectifier diode.
    1 × 4,000 μF electrolytic capacitor, 40 V wkg.

Project 10: PWM controller with speed compensation

The controller of Project 9 lacked feedback, but this can be applied to PWM controllers. Indeed, with PWM, feedback can be used to greatest effect. One of the difficulties in closed-loop controllers is distinguishing between the back EMF generated by the motor and the power delivered by the controller itself. With PWM, however, it is possible to arrange for the feedback to operate *only during the spaces*, so that the signal fed back must have been generated by the motor. But since it would be clearly futile to apply the feedback during the spaces when the transistors are already fully 'off', a delay must be introduced so that the length of the following pulses is modified. Figure 10.1 shows the circuit of Project 9 with a suitable feedback loop added.

The feedback is taken from the output of the controller into a potential divider consisting of R5 and T4. T4 receives base bias from T2 via R6. During the pulses T4 conducts and disables the feedback loop. Between the pulses, however, the feedback loop functions, providing bias for T5, adjustable by VR2. When T5 conducts, it discharges C2 which takes appreciable time to recharge through R1; this introduces the essential element of delay into the

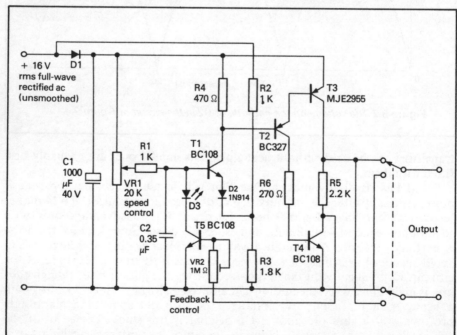

Figure 10.1 *The circuit of Figure 9.1 with speed-compensating feedback.*

operation of the feedback. LED D3 is used in setting VR2. With a train running at moderate speed on level track VR2 should be set so that D3 glows faintly.

Operation of the feedback loop

The 'strobed' feedback consists of pure back EMF (and inductive overshoot but this is of opposite polarity and cannot bias T5). This is roughly proportional to train speed. So motor speeding increases the feedback, biases T5 forward and discharges C2, reducing the control voltage and shortening the pulses. The effect is remarkable. When the train climbs a gradient, D3 glows more faintly and may be extinguished altogether, but the speed is constant. On descending a gradient, D3 glows more brightly, but the speed is still held steady. At high settings of the speed control, when continuous full power is delivered, the feedback loop is disabled and D3 extinguished.

Parts needed
As for Project 9 plus the following:
T4, T5: 2 × BC108 or similar small-signal npn transistor.
R5: 2.2 K resistor.
R6: 270 Ω resistor.
D3: LED (any sort to suit constructor).
C2: 0.33 μF capacitor.
VR2: 1 M pre-set pot.

Part 3

Accessories for controllers

Preamble

The controllers described in Part 2, though capable of giving fine control, are all 'basic' in that they control speed and direction only. Projects 11 to 14 describe a variety of 'add-on' units which enhance the usefulness, interest or safety of controllers. Some of these projects are very simple; others quite complex.

Project 11: LED output indicators

We have all had the experience of turning up the speed control and finding that the train remains stationary. Is it a fault in the controller? Or in the locomotive? Or just dirty track? Here is a very simple device that will tell you whether or not your controller is delivering power. For a single-ended controller (eg, Projects 6, 7, 9 and 10) simply connect an LED (get the polarity right!) with a suitable series resistor (1 K) across the output of the controller *before* the reversing switch. When there is output from the controller the LED will light up and will become brighter as the speed control is advanced. The failure of the LED to light on advancing the control suggests either a fault in the controller or a short circuit on the track.

For bi-directional controllers (eg, Project 8) you will need two LEDs in parallel, cathode to anode. Each protects the other against inverse voltages, but you will still need a series resistor (1 K) to limit the current. The LED that lights will depend on the polarity of the output; you could use a green LED for 'forwards' and a red one for 'reverse'. With certain locos you may find that both LEDs appear to light at once, especially at low settings of the controller. This does *not* indicate a fault in the controller—the effect should vanish on removing the loco from the track. The 'spurious' indication is caused by inductive overshoot from the loco motor: electricity 'stored' in the motor during the pulses is released between the pulses and discharges through the 'reverse' LED, causing it to flash alternately with the 'forward' LED.

Parts needed
1 × LED (2 × LED for bi-directional controller): colour and size to choice of constructor.
1 × 1 K resistor ($\frac{1}{2}$ W).

Project 12: Overload cut-out

Every controller needs some form of overload cut-out to turn the circuit off if excessive current flows through it. Without such a cut-out a short circuit could burn out the output transistors, rectifiers or even the transformer. Many transformer units are fitted with integral thermal overload cut-outs (circuit breakers), which give adequate protection. The simple electronic circuit described in this project also provides suitable protection and will be useful to constructors not having a thermal device or wishing to build an all-electronic controller. The circuit shown in Figure 12.1 is for single-polarity controllers, such as those described in Projects 6, 7, 9 and 10. Cut-outs for dual-polarity controllers, such as that described in Project 8, pose special problems and the author recommends the use of a thermal circuit breaker for that type of controller.

How it works

The current taken by the output stage passes through resistor R1, whose value should be chosen according to the following formula:

$$R1 = \frac{0.68}{I} \, \Omega$$

where I is the current in Amps at which the circuit is to operate; for 1 A—a suitable trip point for most operators—R1 must be 0.68 Ω. If you cannot find one, use three 2.2 Ω resistors (making 0.74 Ω) or four 2.7 Ω (making 0.675 Ω) resistors in parallel. In an overload, the voltage across R1 rises to 0.68 V, bringing T1 into conduction. Pre-set potentiometer VR1 (which may be 5 K, 6.8 K or 10 K) allows for fine adjustment of the trip point. Capacitor C1

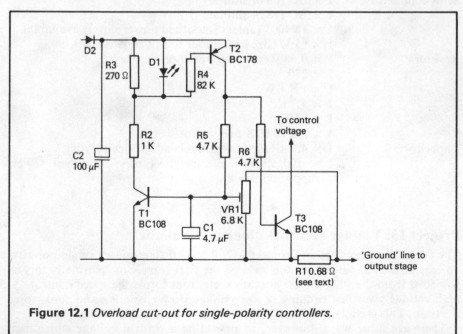

Figure 12.1 *Overload cut-out for single-polarity controllers.*

smooths the input voltage, which is essential on PWM controllers and types operating from unsmoothed supplies.

When T1 conducts, LED D1 lights, indicating overload conditions. T1 also provides base current for T2 which conducts, providing via R5 an alternative source of base current for T1. So both transistors will remain conducting even when the original overload conditions have disappeared. T2 also supplies base current via R6 to T3 whose collector is connected to the base of the first transistor in the controller circuit. When T3 conducts it short-circuits the input to the controller, effectively turning it off.

Resetting the cutout

There are two ways to reset the cutout (after first removing the short circuit or other cause of overload current). Either switch off the power supply to the controller for a few seconds to allow all voltages in the circuit to return to zero. Or momentarily short-circuit the base and emitter of T1 or T2 by means of a suitable push-button switch. (Such a switch, however, holds a hidden danger. It offers the temptation to hold the button down, disabling the cut-out circuit, on occasions when it is operating frequently, eg, when running-in a sticky loco. This is to invite the very type of mishap that the cut-out is intended to prevent.)

As the removal of its power supply resets the cut-out circuit, it must be operated from a *smoothed* power supply—an unsmoothed power supply is effectively switched off 50 or 100 times per second according to the kind of rectification. If the cut-out is being added to a controller having a smoothed power supply (such as those in Projects 9 and 10) D2 and C2 may be omitted.

Parts needed

Semi-conductors:	2 × BC 108 or similar.
	1 × BC 178 or similar.
	1 × 1N4001 (unless smoothed power supply available).
	1 × LED (size and colour to suit constructor).
Resistors:	1 × 0.68 Ω or to suit operator—see text.
	1 × 270.
	1 × 1 K $\frac{1}{2}$ W.
	2 × 4.7 K.
	1 × 82 K.
	1 × 5 K to 10 K pre-set pot.
Capacitors:	1 × 4.7 μF 10 V tantalum bead (or electrolytic).
	1 × 100 μF 25 V electrolytic (unless smoothed power supply available).

Project 13: Voltage control—'inertia simulator'

The controllers described in Projects 6, 7, 9 and 10 all require a single-polarity voltage at their input, ie, on the base of the first transistor. Normally this is provided from the slider of the potentiometer that forms the speed control. A high voltage gives fast running, a low voltage slower running and zero stops the train. This is why we have called this voltage the 'control voltage'.

There are other ways, however, of providing a control voltage which can greatly enhance operator interest. A favourite technique is to use as the control voltage the charge on a high-value capacitor. Separate controls are provided to regulate the rate at which the capacitor charges, the rate at which it discharges and the maximum voltage to which it can be charged. These are called the 'inertia', 'braking' and 'maximum speed' controls respectively. Also needed is a run/slow down function switch, as is an emergency stop switch. These may be separate, or they may be combined as a three-position switch (run/slow down/stop) or they may be combined with the direction control on a five-position switch (run forwards/slow down forwards/stop/slow down reverse/run reverse). Figure 13.1 shows one possible circuit using only a run/slow down and a separate stop switch; it is assumed that a separate direction switch is fitted.

How it works

VR1 is the maximum speed control. The complementary pair T1/T2 transfer the voltage on its slider to control voltage capacitor C1 without passing on the internal resistance of VR1. When the capacitor charges, its charge current passes through inertia control VR2; when it discharges, the discharge current passes through brake control VR3 (or through bypass transistor T3—see later).

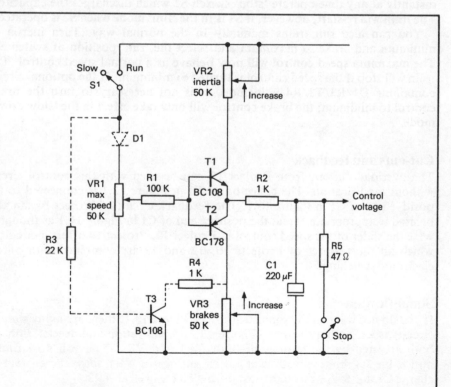

Figure 13.1 *Voltage control system. The components connected by dotted lines are optional (see text).*

Inertia control VR2 regulates the rate at which C1 charges and therefore the acceleration of the train. Set it high (ie, high resistance) for a heavy train, low for a light one. Note that acceleration will also be affected by the setting of VR1.

Brake control VR3 regulates the rate at which the train decelerates when 'slow down' is selected or when the maximum speed control VR1 is turned down. Set it high (nb, low resistance) for rapid deceleration or low for more gradual deceleration. The rate of deceleration will also be affected by the voltage on C1 when 'slow down' is selected. Half an hour's 'play' with the completed circuit will get the operator fully acquainted with the interaction of the controls.

You can now run trains 'semi-automatically' as follows. Select maximum speed, inertia and braking as appropriate. Set switch S1 to 'run'. As capacitor C1 charges, the train will start and will accelerate at a rate determined by the settings of VR1 and VR2 until it reaches the maximum speed determined by VR1. To slow the train set S1 to 'slow down' and the train will decelerate at a rate determined by VR3 until eventually it stops. With the component values as shown in Figure 13.1, and the inertia and brake controls set to maximum *resistance*, the time taken to reach maximum speed from rest or vice versa is about 11 seconds, a useful time on an average layout. To stop the train instantly at any time operate 'stop' switch S2 which discharges the capacitor. The train will re-start, however, if S1 is in the 'run' mode when S2 is operated.

You can also run trains manually in the normal way. Turn inertia to minimum and brake to maximum and select the 'run' position of switch S1. The maximum speed control will now behave as a normal speed control. The train will stop if the speed control is turned to minimum. If the optional circuit containing D1/R3/T3/R4 is included it is not necessary to turn the brake control to minimum; the brake control will only take effect in the 'slow down' mode.

Cut-outs and feedback

The overload cut-out from Project 12 can be used with this control circuit without modification. The collector of T3 in Figure 12.1 is connected to the positive end of C1 in Figure 13.1. The feedback circuit of Project 10 can also be used if appropriate. Treat the positive end of C1 in Figure 14.1 as though it were the slider of the speed control in Project 10. Project 14 offers a circuit in which all the features of Projects 10, 12 and 13 are combined with purely electronic switching.

Simplifications

If you do not want all the sophistication of Figure 13.1, there are many simpler circuits, such as that shown in Figure 13.2. Acceleration and deceleration are both affected by the settings of both VR1 and VR2. You will now find a noticeable lag in acceleration at lower settings of VR1 since the current to charge C1 must flow through most of the VR1 as well as VR2.

Parts needed (complete circuit of Figure 13.1 assumed)
Semi-conductors: 2 × BC 108 or similar.
                          1 × BC 178 or similar.

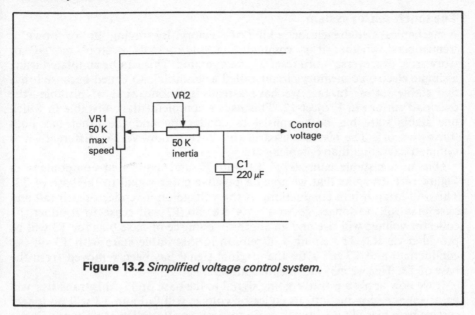

Figure 13.2 *Simplified voltage control system.*

	1 × 1N914 or similar.
	1 × 47 Ω.
Resistors:	2 × 1 K ½ W.
	1 × 22 K.
	1 × 100 K.
Potentiometers:	3 × 50 K.
Switches:	1 × 1 pole 2 way (for run/slow down).
	1 × push button, normally open (for stop).

Project 14: Touch-sensor controller

There can be little in railway modelling more frustrating than a controller with a faulty direction-change or start/stop switch—and no mechanical switch is totally reliable; with use the contacts inevitably wear out. To avoid the use of mechanical switches the author developed a touch-sensor controller in which all switching functions are performed by electronic circuits activated by touch alone. Touch-sensor circuitry, however, offers other advantages besides the novelty and reliability of 'touch' response; these include the possibility of automatic control and are described later.

The controller described here is based on the PWM + feedback circuit of Project 10 with the voltage control circuitry of Project 13, but any PWM controller with voltage control could be adapted. The complete circuit diagram of the author's prototype is given in Figure 14.1. Do not be daunted by its apparent complexity—examining the circuit will reveal the comparatively simple circuit of Project 10 in the centre (T20 to T23), preceded by a complex-looking control circuit (T1 to T15) and followed by a highly modified output section (T27 to T34). In fact there is nothing complicated about the controller at all—it is only an assemblage of several simple circuits. It is straightforward to construct and very rewarding to operate.

The touch-sensor system

A mechanical switch is in fact a kind of memory. By staying 'up' or 'down' it 'remembers' whether it is commanding 'on' or 'off', 'stop' or 'go' or 'forwards' or 'reverse' until reset by the operator. This can be simulated using a simple electronic memory circuit called a 'bistable', so called because it has two stable states. In fact we have already met one kind of bistable—the overload cut-out in Project 12. This uses a complementary bistable in which one stable state has both transistors conducting and the other has both transistors off. The bistable used in this circuit, however, is different—it is symmetrical rather than complementary.

One such bistable consists of T3 and T7 and associated components in Figure 14.1. Imagine that we apply a positive-going signal to the base of T3. This will bring it into conduction, so the voltage on its collector will fall and base bias will no longer go to T7 via R8. So T7 will cease to conduct, its collector voltage will rise and an alternative source of base bias for T3 will be provided via R3. The circuit will remain in this stable state with T3 on (ie, conducting) and T7 off after the original signal has been removed from the base of T3. This we may call the *first* stable state.

If we now apply a positive-going signal to the base of T7, this transistor will be driven into conduction, its collector voltage will fall and T3 will no longer receive base bias via R3, so will cease to conduct. Its collector voltage will rise and an alternative source of base bias for T7 will be provided via R8. So T7 will continue to conduct when the original signal is removed from its base. This we may call the *second* stable state. Therefore the bistable acts as a 'memory' in that it 'remembers' which transistor last received an input signal. Two such bistables are used in this project: T3/T7 controlling the direction-change circuitry and T9/T13 the run/slow-down function.

Touch-sensor control makes use of the conductivity of human skin. When the operator's finger bridges the gap between two adjacent, but separated, contacts—brass screws in the author's prototype (Figure 14.2)—it is momentarily connecting the equivalent of a high-value resistor (a few hundred K) between them. This is more than enough to bias a Darlington pair (eg, T1/T2 and T5/T6) feeding the input of a bistable.

In practice the operator may not even need to bridge the contacts; simply touching the 'live' contact of the pair (ie, that connected to the base of a transistor) will activate the circuit. This 'one-sided' circuit may sound like a breach of the rules of electricity, but it is not. The explanation is that the operator is surrounded by various wires in the room carrying the ac mains supply and he and those wires behave as the plates of a capacitor. The voltage 'picked up' by the operator in this way is small, but when fed via his finger into a Darlington pair and amplified, it is more than sufficient to trip the bistable. Indeed, even without the 'antenna' provided by the operator's finger, the input contacts would pick up enough mains hum to cause problems if the filtering components—the 47 K resistors and 0.01-μF capacitors (R1/C2 etc)— were omitted.

Four sets of touch-sensor contacts are provided, each with its Darlington pair. Those for 'forwards' and 'reverse' activate the respective sides of the direction-change bistable (T3/T7). Reference to Figure 14.1 shows that both these Darlingtons also activate via R11 the 'run' side of the run/slow-down bistable (T9/T13). So touching a set of direction contacts not only specifies the required direction but also starts the train (or sets it accelerating if it had been decelerating in the 'slow-down' mode). The third set of contacts—the 'slow-down' set—simply activates the 'slow-down' side of the run/slow-down bistable. This causes the train to slow down and eventually to stop without affecting the direction selected. The fourth set of contacts is the 'stop' set. This via its Darlington pair and via D11, biases transistor T20 which discharges the control voltage capacitor C6, stopping the train instantly. It also (via D10) activates the 'slow-down' side of the run/slow-down bistable, so the stopped train remains stopped until consciously restarted by the operator touching the appropriate direction contacts.

Of course, a mechanical switch has a toggle or pointer, so you can see which way it is set if in doubt. A touch-sensor circuit similarly needs some visual indication and here LEDs come to the rescue. The author's prototype used three in conjunction with the touch-sensor circuitry: a green one for each direction (D4 and D7) adjacent to the relevant touch sensor contacts and a red one for the 'slow-down' function adjacent to the 'slow-down' contacts, which were in turn adjacent to the 'stop' pair. The series resistors (R4, R9, R18) limit the LED current to a safe 20 mA (with a 22 V supply) while the parallel resistors (R5 and R10) effectively short-circuit the LEDs when they are supposed to be off. Without these resistors the base bias for the transistor that is conducting in the bistable (approximately 250 μA with a 22 V supply) would cause the 'off' LEDs to glow faintly but noticeably. Worse still, this current would bias transistors T4 and T8 on when they are supposed to be off. These transistors, with T10, provide the essential link between the bistables and the controller itself.

Construction

Constructors are advised to have the basic controller (eg, Project 10) and the voltage control system (eg, Project 13) finished and working satisfactorily before proceeding any further. Next construct the touch-sensor control system, ie, T1 to T15, etc. Veroboard or similar is recommended for this part of the circuit as a large number of components may be accommodated in a small space. Having built the control unit, it can be tested without connection to the controller itself, since the LEDs will indicate whether or not the bistables are being activated and that is what matters. The control unit can be tested using two 9 V batteries in series to give an 18 V supply, although the author's prototype was found to work satisfactorily with any supply voltage between 9 V and 22 V. The supply *must*, however, be smoothed and may be operated from the smoothed part of the supply for the Project 10 controller. Full-specification transistors must be used throughout—carefully test all transistors before connecting them in circuit and reject any that show leakage, ie, measurable collector current without base bias.

Little difficulty should be experienced with the circuit. If a bistable persistently stays in one state and refuses to change, increase the value of the resistor between the collector of the transistor that stays off and the base of the transistor that stays on. If that does not cure the fault, check the transistor that stays on and those in the Darlington feeding it and discard any that show leakage; the author had to change several in the prototype. Another malfunction that may only manifest itself later, when the controller is nearly finished, is that of spurious changes of state, eg, a seemingly spontaneous

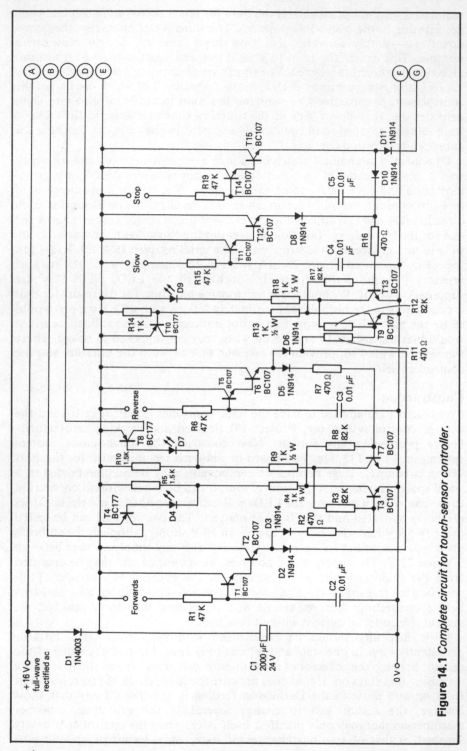

Figure 14.1 *Complete circuit for touch-sensor controller.*

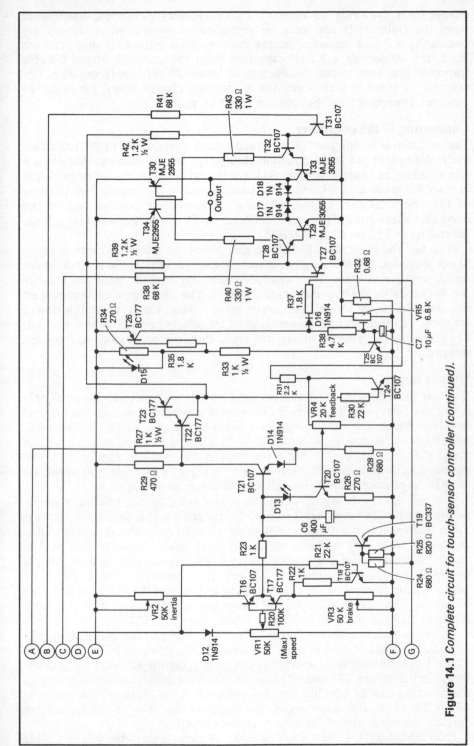

Figure 14.1 *Complete circuit for touch-sensor controller (continued).*

change from 'forwards' to 'reverse'. This is caused by electrical interference from the train itself and may be remedied in several ways. Firstly try connecting a 0.1-μF capacitor across the controller output. If that does not work, try connecting a 0.1-μF capacitor from the collector of the bistable transistor that fails to stay conducting to 'ground', ie, supply negative. For example, if there is a tendency for a spurious change from 'forwards' to 'reverse', connect it from the collector of T3 to 'ground'.

Connecting to the controller

The next step is to link *part* of the touch-sensor control unit to the controller itself. We cannot put in the direction-change system yet, because that needs a totally redesigned output section. So leave the existing direction-change switch in place for the moment. Connect the touch-sensor unit's supply lines to those of the *smoothed* part of the controller. Connect the positive end of the maximum speed control pot to the collector of T10. Add T20 and bias it from the emitter of T15 via D11/R24/R25.

Now test the controller. Switch on and touch the 'stop' contacts at once. Select direction on the original direction-change switch. Select maximum speed, inertia and brake levels as appropriate. To start the train touch either the 'forwards' or the 'reverse' touch contacts. The slow-down LED should go out and the train should accelerate away. Now touch the 'slow-down' contacts. The train should decelerate at a rate selected on the 'brake' control. Try touching the 'stop' contacts; the train should stop at once and remain stopped.

Output stage

One way to achieve bi-directional running with a single-polarity power supply is to use a relay with double-pole changeover contacts to replace the original direction-change switch; the relay coil is energised by a circuit derived from one side of the direction-change bistable. This works well and you can use this method if you like, but we are committed in this book to purely electronic circuits so far as is possible and we are trying in this project to eliminate mechanical contacts with their well-loved tendency to wear out.

A purely electronic way of obtaining a dual-polarity output from a single-polarity supply is to use what is called a bridge circuit. It is called this, because the output spans a ring of four output transistors like a bridge spanning a lake. In fact this is the very 'opposite' of the bridge rectifier circuit (Project 4). The circuit is costly in power transistors, but effective. Only two diagonally opposite transistors are allowed to conduct simultaneously and the choice of opposite pairs determines the polarity of the output and therefore the direction of the train. In Figure 14.1 'forward' movement is provided by T29/T30, both driven by T28 and 'reverse' by T33/T34, both driven by T32.

The pulse-width-modulated output from the original output transistor T23 is fed to the bases of *both* drivers, T28 and T32 via R39 and R42 respectively. Control of direction is by *inhibiting* the driver for the unwanted direction. Inhibitor transistors T27 and T31 receive their base bias from the two sides of the direction-change bistable. So, for example, when 'forwards' is selected, T31 is biased on and short-circuits the input to the 'reverse' driver, leaving only the 'forward' half of the output section operating.

This 'inhibiting' logic is a useful failsafe. A curious operator will be unable to resist the temptation to touch *both* 'forwards' and 'reverse' touch contacts simultaneously, just to see what happens. The answer is that nothing happens. *Both* direction LEDs will light, but *both* output pairs will be inhibited, so there will be no output from the controller at all; no damage will result. If, however, a circuit had been adopted in which the direction-change bistable *enabled* the appropriate output pair, touching both direction contacts would cause a major short circuit across the power supply with all its inherent dangers.

Construction of the output section

This procedure assumes that you are adapting the circuit of Project 10 or some other PWM controller having a pnp output transistor. Remove the original power transistor and replace it with a small-signal pnp type (BC177 or similar). Remove the original direction-change switch. Now you can begin to make up the output unit; tagstrip assembly is recommended as the output transistors do not need heat sinks. The inhibitor transistors T27 and T31 are probably best mounted on the same Veroboard assembly as the main body of the controller circuit. It is a good idea to make up half the output section and test it before making up the other half. For instance, make up T28/T29/T30 and test that. With the 'forwards' circuit activated the train should run forwards, but switching to 'reverse' should stop the train. When this is working satisfactorily, add T32/T33/T34. Check your wiring carefully before switching on. If possible, monitor the current consumed by the controller when checking. Quiescent current (ie, with controls set to minimum) is 40 to 50 mA rising to 150 mA as the speed control is advanced *in the absence of a train*—with a train in circuit you must add its current consumption (typically 100 to 250 mA). These figures assume a 22 V power supply. Switch off at once if there is any build-up of current not accompanied by the running of a train and check the output stage and inhibitor transistors carefully. The completed circuit should give full bi-directional running. The output transistors normally run cool, but may become warm when using locomotives drawing currents exceeding 300 mA.

Feedback and cut-out

The author's prototype incorporated a modified version of the speed-compensating feedback loop described in Project 10. This feedback was applied direct to the control voltage capacitor and acts with a slight delay, which is fascinating to watch. At the start of a descent the train accelerates momentarily and then very noticeably the driver applies the brakes making the descent actually *slower* than the ascent of the same gradient at the same control settings! At high settings of the feedback control it may not be possible to reach full speed—if full speed is needed, turn the feedback control down. The feedback loop is disabled at full speed.

The overload cut-out (T25/T26) is an adaptation of that described in Project 12.

Train-activated control

The bistable 'memories' built into this controller open a host of exciting possibilities to the operator. Because the touch sensors respond to brief impulses, they will respond to stimuli other than the operator's touch. For instance, and this is taking us into the realm of the next section of this book, you could wire reed switches in parallel with the touch contacts. If these are positioned between the rails at strategic spots and if the trains are fitted with magnets to operate the switches, automatic operation is possible.

For instance, you might position a reed switch at the approach to a station out of sight of the operator. This switch would be connected across the 'slow-down' contacts. Provided the controls are suitably set, the train will automatically coast to a halt in the platform without operator intervention. The 'slow-down' LED on the control panel will tell the operator that the 'slow-down' mode has been selected. The 'feedback' LED may give an indication of when the train stops.

For further sophistication you could add another reed switch at the other end of the station wired across the 'stop' touch contacts. Now set the controls so that the train ought to slightly over-run the station. However the new circuit will catch it just in time and ensure that the train stops neatly in the platform.

If the station under consideration is a through station on a single-track line, a two-pole, two-way changeover switch could be incorporated between the two reed switches and the two sets of touch contacts. This would enable the two reed switches to reverse their roles when the train runs in the opposite direction, or else we should have the returning train stopping dead just short of the platform and slowing down as soon as it later tries to leave the station! The operator must, of course, remember to set this switch according to the direction of the train. An 'off' position on the switch, taking both reed switches out of circuit, would allow trains to run through the station without stopping and also provide a remedy for the awful situation of a train stopping with its magnet right over a reed switch, which would otherwise make it impossible to restart the train (without a nudge from an unprototypical hand).

Another use of train-activated control is a 'shuttle service'. Use a single line with a reed switch near each end, one connected to each set of direction contacts. Using a moderate speed, the train will shuttle to and fro indefinitely.

For hints on the use of reed switches and magnets, see Project 15.

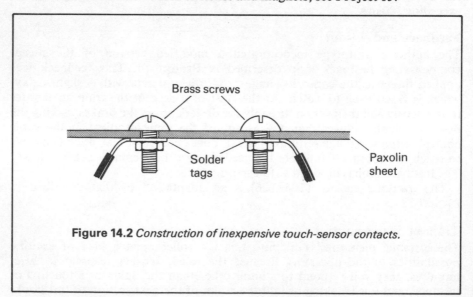

Figure 14.2 *Construction of inexpensive touch-sensor contacts.*

Parts needed for full project (Figure 14.1)

Semi-conductors: 22 × BC 107 (or BC 182 or BC 547).

7 × BC 177 (or BC 212 or BC 557).

1 × BC 337.

2 × MJE 3055 or similar.

2 × MJE 2955 or similar.

1 × 1N4003.

5 × LED, sizes and colours to constructor's taste.

12 × 1N914.

Resistors: 1 × 0.68 Ω (or three 2.2 Ω in parallel).

2 × 270 Ω.

2 × 330 Ω 1 W.

5 × 470 Ω.

2 × 680 Ω.

1 × 820 Ω.

6 × 1 K $\frac{1}{2}$ W.

3 × 1 K.

2 × 1.2 K $\frac{1}{2}$ W.

2 × 1.5 K.

2 × 1.8 K.

1 × 2.2 K.

1 × 4.7 K.

2 × 22 K.

4 × 47 K.

2 × 68 K.

4 × 82 K.

1 × 100 K.

Potentiometers: 1 × 6.8 K pre-set.

1 × 20 K.

3 × 50 K.

Capacitors: 4 × 0.01 μF.

1 × 10 μF 3 V.

1 × 400 μF 24 V.

1 × 2000 μF 24 V.

Miscellaneous: Tagstrips, Veroboard.

Part 4

Train detection systems

Preamble

In Project 14 we saw how the interest and realism of a model railway could be enhanced by the use of train-activated control. Reed switches wired in parallel with the controller's touch-sensor contacts and activated by magnets carried beneath rolling stock gave the facilities of automatic slow-down, stopping and even reversing of trains. Other exciting possibilities such as automatic turnout (points) operation and automatic signalling (both described in Part 5) are feasible given a reliable means of detecting the presence of trains either passing a given point or occupying a given section of track.

In fact train detection is less easy than it sounds. The ingenuity of railway modellers knows no bounds and many systems, some quite bizarre, have been used. The choice of system rests, of course, with the modeller and will be influenced by the nature of the layout, the kind of operations envisaged, the conditions under which it is operated, the exact purpose(s) for which train detection is needed and, one of the most important considerations, whether the train detection system is being added on to an existing layout or built into a new one. As examples of the kinds of factor to be considered, two of the more exotic systems will be considered very briefly indeed.

One system uses 'solar' cells placed on the track. When a train passes over a cell, its electrical output falls. The system has the advantage that any kind of vehicle is detected without modification, but it is expensive and is also affected by the lighting conditions in the room. This system is unsuitable for an operator who enjoys simulating night-time conditions with full loco and coach lighting.

Another system employs weight-operated switches placed beneath the track. Here there are mechanical difficulties. The track must be free to 'sag' as trains pass over it. If the switches have exposed contacts, these are liable to become blocked by dust or stray ballast. But it has the virtue of requiring no modification to rolling stock, except perhaps the addition of extra weight to vehicles which overwise would be too light to activate the switches.

It has long been the author's contention that 'simple is beautiful' and, for this reason, of the three systems described in Projects 15 to 17 none is exotic and none is inordinately expensive; all are reliable. Within these restraints each has its own advantages and disadvantages. The operator considering installing a train detection system is advised to read all three projects and then decide which, if any, is the right one for his layout.

Project 15: Train detection by magnet-operated reed switches

A favourite among railway modellers, this system's great virtue is complete electrical isolation from the track. Reed switches were introduced in Projects 4 and 5, where they formed a part of reed relays, and one application of track-mounted reed switches was mentioned briefly in Project 14, where the switches activated the controller's touch-sensor contacts, giving automatic control. For this sort of application the reed switch is fixed on or beneath the sleepers (ties) and its contacts close momentarily under the influence of a magnet mounted underneath a passing vehicle.

Fitting the reed switches

There are two ways of installing the reed switches and you must decide at the outset which you are going to use as they are not compatible. You can lay them longitudinally along the track half way between the rails—this is the easiest way to install them on an existing layout. You can later disguise them, eg, as ATC ramps. Alternatively—and this the author considers preferable—lay them transversely just beneath the rails. Most miniature reed switches wedge neatly between the sleepers of 00 or H0 track and can be hidden by scattering additional ballast over them.

Fitting the magnets

Much will depend on the sort of magnet you use. Those used by the author are cylindrical, 25 mm long and 6 mm diameter. If you are fitting your reed switches longitudinally, your magnets too must be mounted beneath the vehicles longitudinally and centrally. On many locomotives, especially small tank locos, this poses problems. On tender locos in which the loco itself is powered (and not the tender) the most suitable location will be the tender.

If you are using your reed switches transversely, fitting the magnets will prove far easier. Indeed some locos will not need magnets at all. Some Hornby locomotives are fitted with magnets integral to their chassis to improve adhesion on steel-railed track. Often, but not always, these locos activate transversely-fitted reed switches perfectly satisfactorily without modification. Even locomotives not fitted with adhesion magnets will sometimes activate transverse reed switches. For instance, the author's Lima 'Crab' will—provided it is moving slowly—as the massive magnet in its tender-mounted ring-field motor passes the switch.

Most locos, however, will need to have magnets fitted. There are two methods for use with transverse reed switches. Either one magnet is fitted transversely across the loco at some suitable point on its (or its tender's) frames (Figure 15.1a) or two magnets are fitted vertically, one on each side with their poles in opposite directions (Figure 15.1b). The latter is especially useful in small tank locos, since the magnets can often be fitted just inside the steps to the cab entries. Diesel- and electric-outline models generally present no problems, there being ample space in the battery boxes or elsewhere between the bogies (trucks). If all else fails and you have a loco that seems to offer no suitable location (the Wrenn 2-6-4T is notorious from this point of view), the last resort is to fix the magnet(s) to a van or truck permanently coupled to the loco.

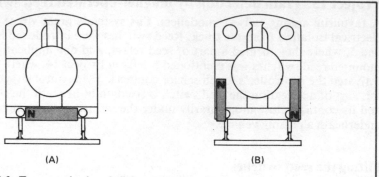

(A)   (B)

Figure 15.1 *Two methods of fixing magnets for use with transverse reed switches.*

Using the system

Because the reed switch contacts are only closed momentarily as the magnet carried by a train passes by, its output consists of a brief pulse (three brief pulses in quick succession when reed switches are fitted longitudinally). For most purposes this pulse is required to initiate a continuous change of state, eg, to select 'slow down' on an automatic controller (as in Project 14) or to change a colour-light signal from green to red (as in Project 18). In Project 15 we saw that one way to use this pulse to effect a change of state is to apply it to the input of a bistable. In that project the reed switch was connected to the bistable via a Darlington amplifier. This was a matter of convenience only, the amplifier being necessary for the touch-sensor operation. The output of a reed switch may be applied direct to the input of a bistable via a suitable current-limiting resistor, as shown in Figure 16.2. A pulse from the reed switch will drive T1 into conduction, after which a 'high' output will be obtained from the collector of T2 and a 'low' output from that of T1. ('High' in this context means 'near supply voltage' and 'low' means 'near zero'.) To reset the bistable the contacts of the reset switch (typically a push-button type) should be closed momentarily, whereupon T2 will be driven into conduction and a 'high' output will be obtained from the collector of T1 and a 'low' output from that of T2.

Section occupation

For many applications—and especially in signalling—we need to know whether there is a train in a given section of line. This can be achieved quite simply by an extension of the circuit shown in Figure 15.2. Imagine that we replace the reset switch by a second reed switch; we shall call this reed switch 2 and the original one reed switch 1. We position reed switch 1 at the beginning of our section and reed switch 2 at the end of it. As a train enters the section it activates reed switch 1, driving the bistable into what we shall call the 'occupied' state. As the train leaves the section, it activates reed switch 2 and the bistable reverts to its original state, which we shall call the 'vacant' state.

It all sounds too simple—and, sure enough, it is, because it only works if all the trains travel in the same direction. If our train were now to reverse back on to the section, it would pass reed switch 2 first, leaving the bistable in its 'vacant' state. If it kept on going, reversing out of the section over reed switch

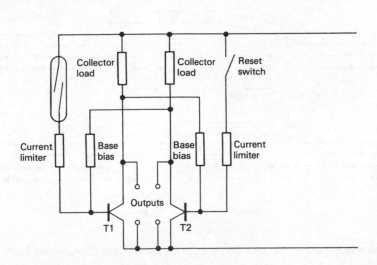

Figure 15.2 *Bistable for converting reed switch output to a steady-state change. For component values see text.*

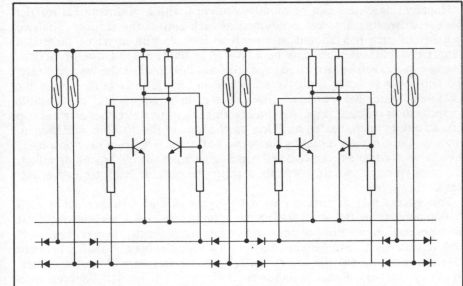

Figure 15.3 *Complete circuit for two adjacent section bistables with shared reed switches. For component values see text. For an alternative value see Figure 19.1.*

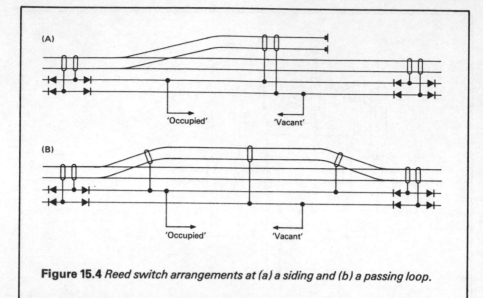

Figure 15.4 *Reed switch arrangements at (a) a siding and (b) a passing loop.*

1, the bistable would now go to its 'occupied' state, even though the section is vacant. However on a double-track line, with wrong-line working absolutely prohibited, this very simple system would be feasible.

Happily this system can be modified to cope with a bi-directional traffic. *Two* reed switches are now positioned at each end of the section. The two switches of each pair should be spaced at least 75 mm apart or there is a danger that both switches may be activated at once, causing a malfunction. The two *outer* switches are wired in parallel and both initiate the 'vacant' state; the two *inner* switches similarly are wired in parallel and both initiate the 'occupied' state. Now imagine that the section is empty and the bistable correctly in its 'vacant' state. A train entering the section *at either end* will trip first an outer switch, having no effect on the state of the bistable, and then an inner switch, correctly initiating the 'occupied' state. The train may now leave the section *at either end*, since it will trip first an inner switch, having no effect, and then an outer switch, correctly turning the bistable back to its 'vacant' state.

This system may at first appear extravagant in reed switches, since each section needs four. But this is only true of an isolated track section; for most purposes sections are not isolated—where one section ends, the next begins. If each section has its own bistable, the reed switch pairs may be shared between adjacent sections, but the 'outer' switch of one section will be the 'inner' switch of the next. For this reason a diode must be inserted between each switch and each bistable input to which it needs to be connected (Figure 15.3). Reference to the figure will show that these diodes prevent switch pulses from being passed down the line to other section bistables where they are not wanted. Figure 15.3 gives the circuit for two section bistables with three pairs of reed switches. An alternative bistable system not needing blocking diodes is described later in Project 19 (see Figure 19.1).

A piece of string has only two ends, but a track section may have more than two. Sidings and passing loops provide means by which a train may clear the main-line section without activating the reed switches at the section ends. Therefore, additional reed switches must be positioned in the sidings and passing loops as shown in Figure 16.4. As these reed switches are not shared with other sections, they are connected direct to the bistable without diodes.

Component values

Deliberately no component values are shown in Figures 15.2 and 15.3, since these will depend on both the supply voltage and the application for which the bistable is intended. If the bistable is only to drive other circuits, eg, the electric turnout motor driver circuit (Project 22), a low collector current (eg, around 3 mA) will be sufficient. If the bistable is to drive two-aspect colour-light signals direct (Project 21) a higher current will be needed; 30 mA is recommended. The following table gives recommended component values for low- and high-current bistables over a range of supply voltages. Power supplies must be smoothed.

Supply voltage	Low current (3 mA)			High current (30 mA)		
	Collector load	Base bias	Switch limiter	Collector load	Base bias	Switch limiter
6 V	1.8 K	180 K	82 K	180 Ω	18 K	8.2 K
9 V	2.7 K	270 K	150 K	270 Ω	27 K	15 K
12 V	3.9 K	390 K	180 K	390 Ω	39 K	18 K
16 V	4.7 K	470 K	220 K	470 Ω	47 K	22 K
22 V	6.8 K	680 K	330 K	680 Ω	68 K	33 K

Parts needed (per bistable)

Semi-conductors:	2 × BC 108 or similar npn transistor.
Resistors:	2 × collector load.
	2 × base bias.
	2 × switch limiter (see above table for values).
Miscellaneous:	Reed switches.
	Diodes (type 1N914 or similar).
	Magnets for rolling stock.
	Veroboard or tagstrip.

Project 16: Isolated sections and check rails

The one main disadvantage of reed switches and magnets as a train detection system (Project 15) is that it demands modification both of the track (installing the reed switches) and of the locomotives or other vehicles to be detected (installing the magnets). Although the systems described in this project both involve extensive modification of the track, no modification of locomotives is needed.

Isolated sections

Each locomotive picks up power from at least two wheels on each side. So, if you take a short length of rail—say 20 mm—and isolate it using insulated fish-

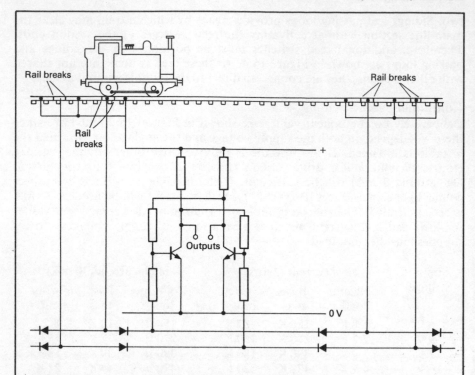

Figure 16.1 *Circuit of section bistable with shared isolated sections (or check rails). For component values see the text of Project 15.*

plates or by plugging the gaps with epoxy resin, a loco running over the isolated section will momentarily turn that section 'live' when one pick-up wheel is in contact with the section and another is in contact with the main 'live' rail.

The isolated section can be connected to the input of a bistable (Figure 16.1). As the figure shows, the live rail and isolated sections replace the reed switches in Project 15; apart from this the circuitry is identical to that of the previous project. The 'live' rail must be connected to the positive supply for the bistable—this could cause difficulties on a layout incorporating a reverse loop or a triangular junction.

Of course, every system has its disadvantages. With this system the penalty is that of having large numbers of 'dead' sections, making the locomotives more prone to stalling. If you use this system it is wise to fit locomotives with additional power pick-ups if possible and it is even more important than normal to keep the track and locomotive wheels scrupulously clean.

The isolated sections should be as short as possible and on no account longer than the shortest electrical wheelbase (ie, distance between first and last power-pick-up-fitted wheels) in your loco stud; on a motorised Airfix 'Pug' this is only 24 mm. Other vehicles besides locomotives will be detected if they are fitted with power pick-ups on at least two wheels on each side. Coaches fitted with lighting units, for instance, will be detected.

Check rails

A check rail is a short length of rail mounted just inside the regular running rail and intended on prototype railways either to limit speed on tight curves (by friction with the wheel flanges) or on turnouts (points, switches) or crossovers to hold the wheel in contact with the running rail where there is a gap in the opposite running rail. In train detection, however, a check rail may serve a different purpose.

A check rail may take the place of an isolated section in the system just described. This offers the advantages that i) there are no 'dead sections', ii) any metal wheel will activate the system and iii) the system is easy to install on existing layouts. The only disadvantage is the unsightliness of the check rails themselves—in 00/H0 layouts they are generally about 75 mm long. Even so, they need not be prominent. At exhibitions it is doubtful whether check rails would be noticed by casual spectators, especially if positioned inside the running rail nearest the audience.

Positioning of the check rails is important. There must be sufficient clearance for the coarsest wheels in use on the layout, but then the finest wheels may not contact the check rail. Obviously the modeller must be prepared to experiment, especially if wheels of different standards are in use on the layout.

Parts needed
As for Project 15, but omit reed switches and magnets.

Project 17: Track circuits (EDOTIS)

A number of track circuit units are available commercially. These provide a method of train detection that requires no modifications whatever to locomotives and little, if any, to track. EDOTIS (Electronic Detection Of Trains In Sections), manufactured by Rugby Engineering Services, was developed by the author as a highly improved version of the simple signalling system described in Project 4. All the commercial systems, however, work on the same principles.

EDOTIS is simple, accurate and reliable. Like the earlier system its only requirement is that the track sections are electrically isolated in one rail at least, each therefore having its own feed from the controller(s). If your layout is already divided into sections for cab control and you are willing to use these sections also for signalling, no further modification is needed.

EDOTIS simulates the track circuitry of prototype railways within the radically different electrical confines of model railways. On prototype railways the track sections are electrically isolated and a low voltage is applied between the rails. A relay coil is also connected between the rails and, under normal conditions with the section vacant, is energised by the voltage. The wheel/axle assemblies of prototype railway vehicles are electrically conductive, so if there are any vehicles in the track section, the relay coil is short-circuited. The opening and closing of the relay contacts therefore give 'occupied' and 'vacant' indications, which may be used to light a lamp in a mimic diagram or provide interlocks on a manual signalling system or may be linked directly into an automatic signalling system.

Of course, this kind of track circuit cannot be used on a two-rail model railway for two reasons. Firstly, the rails already form part of the circuit that provides the power for the locomotive. The power circuit and the track circuit would inevitably interfere with each other causing short circuits and spurious indications. Secondly, although track circuit current might pass through a model locomotive, most other rolling stock of necessity has insulated wheels and would not 'show up' in a track circuit.

Happily neither of these difficulties is insurmountable. The best philosophies advocate turning enemies into friends and that is what an EDOTIS unit does with the conflicting currents in the track: it makes the power voltage serve also as the track circuit voltage and monitors the current flowing from the controller into the track section.

Now one of the difficulties of using the controller output as the track circuit voltage is that it is not dependable. When the controller is turned to 'stop', for instance, its output voltage disappears and the track circuit is disabled. This, you may remember, was one of the shortcomings of the simple signalling system in Project 4. That circuit overcame the difficulty by a far-from-subtle technique—in the absence of controller output it turned the signal red, even if the line was clear, but EDOTIS is more sophisticated. From its own power supply it injects an auxiliary current into the track enabling current monitoring to continue in the absence of controller output, so that accurate 'occupied' and 'vacant' indications are given continuously. The auxiliary current, of course, must be kept very low to ensure that, when the controller is turned to 'stop', trains cannot run. In practice it is generally between $100\,\mu A$ and $400\,\mu A$.

The second difficulty regarding the insulated wheels of rolling stock disappears if you wish to detect only locomotives and for most purposes this will suffice. If you insist on detecting other rolling stock you can, but you must arrange for these vehicles to draw current from the track. Any already fitted with lights operating from the controller output will probably need no further modification. Others must be fitted with power pick-ups connected to a suitable resistor. This should have the highest resistance that will activate the EDOTIS units on your layout and will have to be found by experiment, since this is affected by many factors including the internal resistance of the controller in use. Touch the leads of a variety of resistors across the track trying all settings of the controller. An alternative for vehicles fitted with metal-tyred wheels and metal axles only insultated by plastic spokes or a rubber bush is to paint over the insulant with electrically conductive silver paint. This may give initially an embarrassingly low resistance, but it can be raised to a suitable level by brushing or scratching the paint away when dry. If you have trains of permanently coupled vehicles, you need only 'conductivise' the first and last vehicles of the train.

A practical EDOTIS unit

The heart of an EDOTIS unit is its current-monitoring system. The simple signalling circuit of Project 4 used a reed relay, but that is not feasible in an EDOTIS unit because the reed relay cannot respond to the tiny 'auxiliary' current, which must be small to prevent unwanted movement of trains; if the coil were made larger to increase the sensitivity of the relay, its resistance would cause an intolerable voltage loss between controller and track.

Figure 17.1 gives the circuit of a practical EDOTIS unit. The current

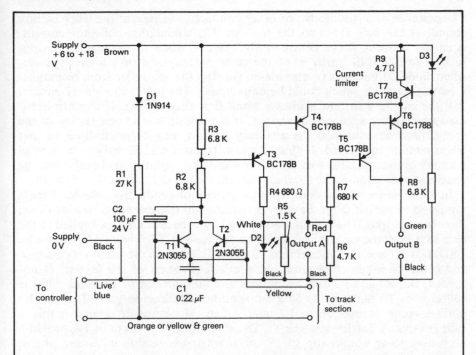

Figure 17.1 *Circuit diagram of EDOTIS, a track circuit system. Colours are the colour coding of the flying leads used on the commercial version.*

detector consists of the pair of transistors T1/T2, the base of each being connected to the emitter of the other. Power from the controller to the track section is applied to this pair of base/emitter junctions; which junction it passes through depends, of course, on the polarity. These transistors must be power types, since more than 1 A may on occasion be passed; power dissipation, however, is minimal so heat sinks are not needed. Voltage loss between controller and track is always one 'diode drop' of 0.7 V, which has no noticeable effect on the performance of trains, except that worn-out locomotives consuming 1 A or so may run a little more slowly.

The collectors of T1/T2 are bonded and connected via a resistor network to the positive side of the EDOTIS unit's power supply which is returned to the *live* side of the controller output. Analysis of this configuration will show that the passage of current of either polarity into the section will cause collector current to flow in R2/R3; this collector current will, however, be constant in polarity. This is an unusual application of transistors in that a large base bias (typically 250 mA) controls a small collector current (typically about 600 μA with a 9 V supply). The transistors also respond to much smaller base bias currents; the auxiliary current when the controller is off is typically 130 μA and a large proportion of this may be shunted through feedback loops in the controller.

The auxiliary current is provided via diode D1 and resistor R1 from the positive side of the power supply to the 'earth' side of the controller output.

The presence of a locomotive or other conductive vehicle in the track section completes the bias chain to the base of T2, stimulating collector current. Auxiliary current flows continuously, except when the controller output relative to EDOTIS 'earth' is of the same polarity and of a higher voltage, when diode D1 becomes reverse biased (to stop the controller from recharging a battery, if used, which could be dangerous). The high value of R1 ensures that the auxiliary current is always small (less than 1 mA). If a controller is used which gives a smooth dc output, it is possible that at one setting of the speed/direction control(s) the auxiliary current may be neutralised so that trains remain undetected. If this happens, connect a 12 K resistor in parallel with the output transistor of the controller. The resulting 'leakage' from the controller will 'swamp' the auxiliary current and ensure consistent detection.

In the presence of a locomotive, short circuit or conductive vehicle, there is always *some* output from the current detector; in the absence of any of these, there is no output. The output is smoothed by capacitor C2 and applied to the base of T3, whose emitter is coupled to the base of T4. Figure 17.1 shows an LED (D2) in the collector circuit of T3. This lights when the section is occupied and could be mounted remotely in a mimic diagram of the layout. If not needed, D2, R4 and R5 may be omitted and the collector of T3 bonded to the collector of T4 making T3/T4 a conventional Darlington pair. T4 provides positive-going output (up to 100 mA) when the section is *occupied*; this is called output A. Darlington pair T5/T6 driven from the output of T4, provides a positive-going output (up to 100 mA) when the section is *vacant*; this is called output B.

The circuitry around T7 is optional and could be omitted, the emitters of T4 and T6 being returned direct to the positive side of the power supply. T7 is fitted in commercial EDOTIS units to protect T4 and T6 against burn-out if the outputs should be short-circuited. T7 is biased to provide a maximum collector current of 100 mA; T4 and T6 form its collector load. LED D3 does not light up—it is used only as a voltage reference in the base circuit of T7 and could be replaced by a pair of small-signal silicon diodes (1N914 or similar) in series. Construction should present no difficulties. Veroboard or tagstrip assembly may be used.

Power supply

An EDOTIS Unit needs a 6 V to 18 V dc smoothed power supply, which *must* be separate from that of the controller since, as mentioned previously, the 'live' side of the controller output (if distinguished) must be connected to the 'earth' side of the EDOTIS power supply. A 9 V battery (PP9 or similar) may be used. Where several EDOTIS units monitoring various sections are connected to the output of the same controller, they may share the same power supply. If more than one controller is in use on a layout, a separate supply must be used in conjunction with each controller to power the EDOTIS units monitoring the sections fed from it. Where a switch is provided so that sections (via their EDOTIS units) may be operated from a choice of controllers, this switch must also select the appropriate power supply for the EDOTIS unit; a two-pole switch may be used selecting the 'live' side of the controller and the positive side of the EDOTIS power supply. The negative side of the power supply may be returned direct to the 'live' side of the controller to which it relates.

Testing and use of the EDOTIS unit

Connect the completed EDOTIS unit to a track section and power supply as described above. With a locomotive in the section LED D2 should be on at all settings of the controller. With the loco removed the LED should be off at all settings of the controller. Spurious output (ie, the LED lighting in the absence of a loco) especially with the controller on full may be caused by electrical interference (eg, mains leads in close proximity to the track), dampness in the track or partial short circuits (especially on track made from rails soldered to copper-clad-board sleepers—small particles of copper in the insulating breaks have caused spurious indications when using EDOTIS; although not with the particular circuit described here.) Experiment with C1 if you suspect electrical interference and try automotive water repellent on the track for damp problems. Non-indication (ie, failure of the LED in the light in the presence of a loco) is usually due to dirty track or bad contacts in the loco itself.

There is a built-in time delay (set by C2/R2) of about $\frac{3}{4}$ second in the change from the 'occupied' (ie, output at A) to the 'vacant' (ie, output at B) indication. This is deliberate—it helps to ensure that on dirty track where a locomotive is only picking up power intermittently, but kept moving by its own momentum, EDOTIS gives a continuous 'occupied' indication rather than an intermittent one. So a colour-light signal driven from the EDOTIS unit will give a steady red (or yellow)—nothing looks more pathetic than a colour-light signal alternating erratically between aspects!

The main use of EDOTIS is in signalling. Two-aspect colour-light signals can be driven direct from its outputs (Projects 18 and 21). With additional circuitry three-aspect, four-aspect and semaphore signals can be driven (Projects 19 to 22). EDOTIS can be used for other applications, eg, automatic control, but the variable relationship of its 'earth' potential to that of the controller introduces complications. It may be necessary to employ a relay or an opto-isolator* as an 'interface' between the EDOTIS output and the controller input. EDOTIS detects the presence of a train *in a section* rather than at one point, but detection by EDOTIS at one point can be achieved by introducing a special short section; this must, however, be long enough to ensure that current is drawn in it.

Parts needed

Semi-conductors:	2 × 2N3055 or similar high-current npn transistors.
	5 × BC 178B or simillar small-signal, high-gain pnp transistors.
	1 × 1N914 or similar small-signal diode.
	2 × LED colour and size to 'taste'.
Capacitors:	1 × 0.22 µF.
	1 × 100 µF 24 V wkg.
Resistors:	1 × 4.7 Ω. 3 × 6.8 K.
	1 × 680 Ω. 1 × 27 K.
	1 × 1.5 K. 1 × 680 K.
	1 × 4.7 K. Circuit board or tagstrip.

*An opto-isolator is a semi-conductor device consisting of an LED and a light-sensitive transistor (sometimes a Darlington pair) enclosed in a light-proof package. Light from the LED is used instead of base bias to stimulate collector current in the transistor. The useful feature of an opto-isolator is the electrical isolation between the 'bias' applied to the LED and the transistor circuit, so that differences of potential between the two circuits are unimportant.

Part 5

Automatic signalling and turnout (points) control

Preamble

If you are one of those modellers whose delight is a massive bank of levers operating a host of turnouts (points) and semaphore signals by means of an incredible network of mechanical linkages and whose chief joy consists in setting up a route on the turnouts and then setting the signals appropriately by hand, you may well be advised to give Part 5 a miss. It is intended for those modellers who, like the author, lack the skill and patience to set up painstakingly a complex mechanical array or lack the capital to do so. Moreover some of us, even if we set it up, would get confused when we tried to operate it.

Much of Part 5 is devoted to the automatic operation of colour-light signals. For this the author makes no excuses. The book, after all, is on the applications of electronics to railway modelling and electronics can make a greater contribution to automatic colour-light signalling than it can to other forms of signalling or turnout control (although these are described). If excuses are needed, there is no shortage of them. Colour-light signals are far simpler to set up and use than semaphore types: moreover they are not—as some modellers mistakenly believe—a recent innovation only appropriate on modern-image layouts. The first installation of colour-light signals on a main line in the UK was in 1924 on the former Great Central line between Marylebone and Neasden in connection with special services operating to the Empire Exhibition at Wembley. The first four-aspect installations were on the Southern Railway in the late 1920s. All four pre-nationalisation companies had some colour-light signals before the Second World War so they are not out of place in layouts depicting 'the Big Four' or British Railways steam era.

There are two sorts of colour-light signals.

Searchlight signals have a single colourless lens; the colour shown (the *aspect*) is changed by means of a slide between the lamp and the lens moved by solenoids. Some searchlight signals are fitted with repeaters below the main signal head. On the LNER main line near York at one time three-aspect searchlight signals were operated as four-aspect by the addition of a yellow light above the main signal head. Model searchlight signals generally operate on the light-transmission principle; coloured bulbs in the base of the signal send their light up a light guide in the post of the signal to the signal head.

Multiple-lens signals have a separate lens for each colour (aspect); generally the lenses are 8 inches (203 mm) in diameter and 1 foot (305 mm) apart. These are usually modelled using coloured 'grain-of-wheat' bulbs. Those in the excellent 'Eckon' range of signal kits for 00 scale are 3.5 mm in diameter, slightly larger than scale although this is not very noticeable in the finished model.

A *two-aspect signal* displays two colours (aspects) only. Two-aspect colour-light signalling is sometimes a direct replacement for older semaphore units. A 'home' signal guarding a section or a junction displays green when the line is clear and red at other times. A 'distant' signal is a repeater, giving the train driver advance warning of the indication currently shown by the next home signal. Its aspects are amber (always called yellow by railwaymen) if repeating a red, and green if repeating a green. In three- or four-aspect areas the last signal on the approach to a terminus is a two-aspect type showing red if the approach is not clear and *yellow* if it is. This yellow is a 'distant' warning of the buffers at the end of the line, which are regarded as a permanently red signal. In two-aspect signals the more restrictive aspect is generally positioned below the other.

A *three-aspect signal* combines the functions of home and distant two-aspect types. Red, as on a home signal, means 'stop—the next section is not clear'. Yellow, as on a distant signal, means 'caution—the next signal is red'. Green means 'proceed—the next two sections are clear'.

Four-aspect signalling was first introduced on the Southern Railway on lines required to carry both intensive suburban passenger traffic and fast express services. To accommodate minimal-headway low-speed services the length of the sections must be kept short, but then an express train, passing a three-aspect signal showing yellow, would have only one short section length in which to stop, which would be insufficient (except by the application of emergency braking which would cause discomfort to passengers). Hence the introduction of the fourth aspect: double yellow which means 'caution—the next-but-one signal is red'. This gives the driver two sections in which to stop his train, which is adequate even for the fastest trains. Green on a four-aspect signal means 'proceed—the next three sections are clear'. Red and yellow, of course, have the same meanings as on two- and three-aspect signals. In a four-aspect area the last-but-one signal before a terminus is a three-aspect type which displays red, yellow or double yellow. Since the next-but-one signal is the 'permanently red' buffer stop, a green indication would be inappropriate. Sometimes a standard four-aspect signal head is used with a white blanking disc in place of the green.

Both searchlight and multiple-aspect signals can be modelled using LEDs. Although the author has constructed model searchlight signals in which separate sub-miniature LEDS were mounted inside a massive signal head, the construction of model searchlight signals is made much easier by the availability of multicolour LEDs. Some of these give realistic deep red, yellow and green and Project 26 describes the construction of a signal using this technique. Results are superior to the light-transmission-type signals available commercially. Project 4 described the construction of a simple two-aspect signal using LEDs; similar techniques can be used to model three- and four-aspect types. It is also possible to substitute 3 mm LEDs for the 3.5 mm bulbs used in some proprietary model signals. LEDs offer several advantages over filament lamps. These include lower current consumption, cool running, unlimited life (if used properly) and—not least—better colour. A miniature tungsten lamp has only a thin envelope of glass which can be pigmented, whereas an LED has a solid plastic envelope, giving a deeper and more realistic colour.

Projects 18 to 20 will describe signalling using lamps and Projects 21 and 26 signalling using LEDs because of the differences in operation between signals using lamps and those using LEDs.

Project 18: Two-aspect signalling using bulbs

The bistables used in the train detection systems described in Projects 15 and 16 and the EDOTIS unit described in Project 17 can all drive two-aspect signals fitted with miniature bulbs (eg, signals constructed from 'Eckon' kits) without any additional circuitry. If you are using bistables, remove the collector load resistors from the transistors and wire the bulbs in their place. The red bulb (yellow in a distant signal) must, of course, be connected to the transistor that becomes conductive when the section is occupied. Be careful about the supply voltage. The manufacturer of 'Eckon' signals recommends the use of a 12 V supply and the insertion of a 220 Ohm resistor (supplied with the kit) in series with the signal; this cuts down the heat generated by the bulb, which otherwise might cause distortion of the polystyrene signal head. If you use a 12 V supply, return the leads from the two bulbs to the positive supply line via the resistor. Alternatively, operate the bistable from a 6 V or 9 V supply and omit the resistor; the author has found that this gives adequate lighting without heating problems. Using a lower voltage also prolongs the life of the bulbs. For signalling using bulbs do not use supplies over 12 V.

Typical current consumption of a bulb is 35 mA (from either 12 V with resistor or 9 V without). If the lighting seems feeble and the current proves to be less than 35 mA, reduce the value of the bias resistors in the bistable. A suitable value for 9 V or 12 V supplies in this application is 12 K to 15 K. Reduce the switch limiter resistor to 6.8 K.

Each bistable should be capable of driving two such signals, the bulbs being connected in parallel. Do not exceed two signals with the transistors specified or you may exceed the 100 mA maximum collector current rating of the BC 108 and similar types. If you must run more than two signals from one bistable replace the transistors with a more robust type, eg, BC 337 (500 mA maximum). You may need to lower the associated resistor values further.

If you use EDOTIS this is even easier. Simply connect the red lamp (yellow in a distant signal) to output A and the other to output B. If you use a 12 V supply return the lamps to negative via the resistor. Alternatively, as before, use a 6 V or 9 V supply and omit the resistor.

All of the other remarks about bistables apply equally to EDOTIS although no difficulty should be experienced with inadequate light, even with two signals being driven. If you want to drive more than two signals you will need to replace the output transistors with type BC 327 or similar and omit the current limiter (T7), taking the emitters of the new T4 and T5 straight to the positive supply.

Manual over-ride

On prototype automatic signalling systems in the UK the law demands that a minimum number of signals (usually 1 in 4) be fitted with a manual over-ride, ie, a means whereby a signalman can turn the signal red, even though the line is clear. (In a multiple-aspect area the signal(s) before that turned manually red will show yellow aspect(s) as appropriate.) This provides a means whereby in emergency, eg, landslide or bridge damaged, trains can be stopped before running into danger.

This facility can be easily modelled. Simply connect a switch between the collector of the output transistor driving the red aspect and the negative supply of the bistable or the positive supply of the EDOTIS unit. This short-circuits the 'red' output transistor and removes the bias from the other. In EDOTIS units the train detection facility is not lost—LED 1 will continue to light only when the section is occupied.

Parts needed
Signals as required.
Bistables or EDOTIS units as required (see Projects 15 to 17).

Project 19: Three-aspect signalling using bulbs

Whether you are using bistables or EDOTIS units or some other system of train detection, there are several effective and reliable methods of three-aspect operation. Oddly some are *simpler* than the corresponding two-aspect system. Three systems are described here. Throughout these descriptions references to *section 1* (bistable 1 or EDOTIS 1) relate to the section beginning immediately beyond the signal under consideration; *section 2*, etc, relates to the section beyond that, and so on.

Method 1—'Complementarity'

The bistables described in Projects 15 and 16 all used npn transistors and Project 18 described how signal lamps could be connected between their collectors and the positive supply line for two-aspect signalling. It would be equally possible and no more expensive to use pnp transistors and to connect the lamps between the collectors and the negative supply line. All diodes, of course, would need to be reversed. Moreover we could, if we wished, alternate the bistables so that bistable 1 uses npn transistors, bistable 2 pnp types, bistable 3 npn types and so on.

This may sound far-fetched, but there is much to commend the idea. Figure 19.1 shows two such 'complementary' section bistables, the first using npn and the second pnp transistors. Note that i) the blocking diodes and half the switch limiting resistors are eliminated, saving costs and space and ii) three-aspect signals can be driven direct. The red aspect is wired direct between collector and supply as in two-aspect signalling—its operation is conditional only on the occupancy of section 1. Both yellow and green aspects are wired to the collector of the other transistor in bistable 1; they are returned via the collectors of the two transistors in bistable 2. Some consideration of the circuit will show that the logic is correct for three-aspect signalling. Note the blocking diode in series with the yellow aspect. This is essential. Without it, when T2 of bistable 1 is off and T2 of bistable 2 is on, a circuit is completed via the red aspect of signal 2 and the green and yellow aspects of signal 1. Not only would this cause the three lamps to glow faintly, but the current consumption of

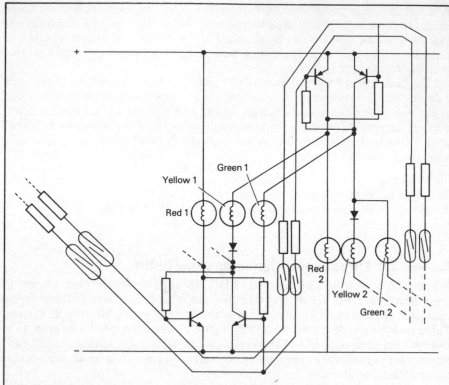

Figure 19.1 *'Complementarity' bistables in use for three-aspect signalling.*

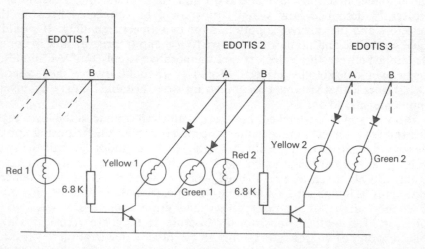

Figure 19.2 *'Complementarity' system for three-aspect signalling using EDOTIS—two sections shown. Note the additional blocking diode in series with the green aspect to prevent the transistor from receiving bias from output A via the yellow and green aspects.*

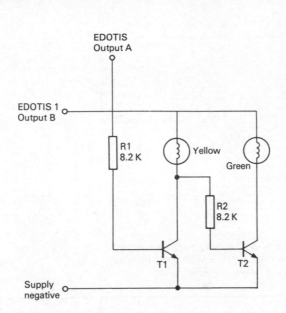

Figure 19.3 *'Slave' driver circuit for the yellow and green aspects of a three-aspect signal.*

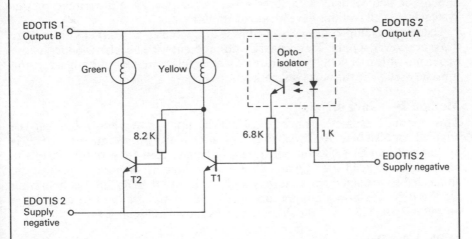

Figure 19.4 *Use of an opto-isolator to couple a 'slave' driver to an EDOTIS unit operating from a different power supply.*

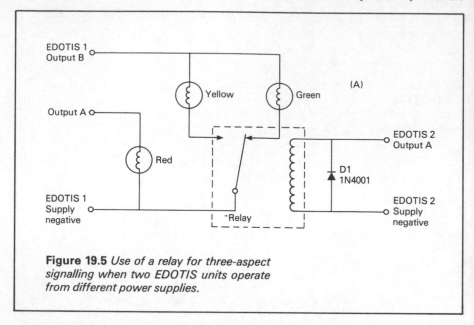

Figure 19.5 *Use of a relay for three-aspect signalling when two EDOTIS units operate from different power supplies.*

filament lamps under these conditions is remarkably high and transistors may become overloaded for reasons that are not immediately apparent.

The EDOTIS unit described in Project 17 uses pnp output transistors, but units could be constructed with npn output transistors, so that it would be possible to alternate pnp-output and npn-output units along the lines as with bistables. However, the same effect can be achieved by adding one npn transistor biased from output B; Figure 19.2 shows in simplified form the circuit for two sections with three-aspect signalling. One advantage of this system is that all sections have identical circuitry.

The above examples have assumed that the bistables or EDOTIS units share the same power supply. This is usually no problem with bistables, but can pose problems with EDOTIS. If separate power supplies are used, another method must be used—see the next two methods.

Method 2—'Slave drivers'

This method assumes the use of EDOTIS units throughout, but can be adapted for bistables. A 'slave driver' is made up using npn transistors. This is a 'dummy' npn EDOTIS output, its input being taken from output A of the pnp-output EDOTIS 2. Figure 19.3 shows how it operates. It must be connected to the same power supply as EDOTIS 1. If EDOTIS 2 is operating from a different power supply, an opto-isolator may be used to couple the output of EDOTIS 2 into the slave driver, as shown in Figure 19.4.

Method 3—Relays

A low-voltage relay having at least one set of changeover contacts may be used to select the yellow and green aspects in three-aspect installations, as shown in Figure 19.5. One advantage is that differences between power supplies cause no complications. The diode in parallel with the relay coil is to prevent inductive overshoot when the coil is de-energised from damaging the output transistor. In fact the author has never fitted the diode and has never had any difficulties with overshoot pulses from relay coils, but 'good design practice' is to include it.

Parts needed
EDOTIS units or bistables as necessary (see text).
Slave driver components as necessary (see text).
Opto-isolators or relays.
Signals.

Project 20: Four-aspect signalling using bulbs

Regrettably opportunities to use four-aspect signalling on model railways are few, because authentic use of the system demands at least four sections in sequence, each long enough to contain a train of reasonable length. For the benefit, however, of readers fortunate or ambitious enough to install such a system—or just curious— here is a system which the author developed for use with EDOTIS. It is, of course, a prerequisite that EDOTIS units be installed on three consecutive sections, called here sections 1, 2 and 3, section 1 being the one that begins immediately beyond the signal being driven. The circuit is shown in Figure 20.1.

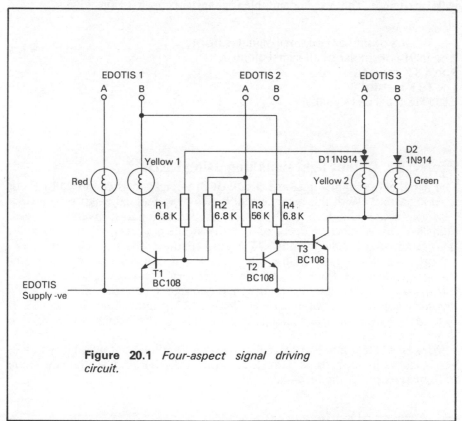

Figure 20.1 *Four-aspect signal driving circuit.*

The red aspect is driven, as in two- and three-aspect systems direct from the A output of EDOTIS 1. Aspect yellow 1 is derived from output B of EDOTIS 1, but can only light when transistor T1 is on. This has alternative sources of bias from the A outputs of both EDOTIS 2 and 3. Thus this aspect is correctly illuminated when section 1 is vacant and there is a train in either sections 2 or 3.

Transistor T3 is so biased that it is only on when both sections 1 and 2 are vacant. Its bias is derived from the B output of EDOTIS 1 but is short-circuited to ground by T2 when section 2 is occupied. So, when sections 1 and 2 are both vacant T3 conducts and either yellow 2 or green lights, depending on the occupancy of section 3. Blocking diodes D1 and D2 in series with yellow 2 is essential. If, as is likely, a red aspect is wired from output A of EDOTIS 3 to ground, under certain conditions a circuit would be completed via this, yellow 2 and green, leading to a heavy current drain and danger of overloading; D1 blocks this current drain.

This circuit was developed for use with EDOTIS and the author has not tested it with bistables. Bistables have a leakage current via their bias resistors. If this circuit were used with pnp bistables (or a pnp version of this circuit were tested with npn bistables) it would probably be necessary to add resistors (value to be determined by experiment—suggest 1.2 K) from the base of each transistor to 'ground' to prevent spurious activation of the transistors by the leakage current. The circuit is suitable for tagstrip construction.

Parts needed
3 × BC 108 or similar npn small-signal transistor.
2 × IN914 or similar small-signal diode.
3 × 6.8 K resistor.
1 × 56 K resistor.
EDOTIS units and signals.

Project 21: Colour light signalling using LEDs

The signal in the simple signalling circuit of Project 4 consisted of two LEDs in reverse parallel. With this arrangement a two-aspect signal needs only a two-wire connection and each LED protects its partner against inverse voltages. Signals of this type can be operated direct from the outputs of section bistables (Projects 15 and 16) and from EDOTIS units (Project 17).

With bistables choose resistor values for a collector current of 30 mA and simply connect the leads to the signal between the collectors of the two transistors. If you wish to drive more than one signal, connect the extra signals *in series* with the first, not in parallel. With a 12 V supply, four such signals in series may be driven. If a signal persistently shows the wrong aspect, reverse the connections to it.

With EDOTIS connect the signal(s) between the 'live' outputs, but you will need to add suitable resistors from the outputs to 'ground'. Calculate the value of these resistors by the formula:

$$R = \frac{V - 2n}{15} \; K$$

where V is the supply voltage and *n* the number of signals in series. Thus to operate 3 signals from a 12 V supply R = 6/15 = 0.4 K. The nearest preferred value is 390 Ω.

For three- and four-aspect signalling it is best to use the same circuits as for bulbs. You will need to add series resistors (value = $\frac{V-2}{15}$ K) and to watch the polarity of the LEDs. Where a blocking diode is specified in the circuit using bulbs it is even *more* necessary with LEDs for at this point the LED would otherwise be subjected to severe inverse voltages. Leakage currents can cause LEDs to glow perceptibly when supposed to be off. Spurious glow can usually be killed by adding a resistor (1.5 K is generally suitable) in *parallel* with the offending LED.

Parts needed
LEDs, bistables, EDOTIS units, resistors, diodes; see text.

Project 22: Semaphore signalling and turnout (points) operation

There are two ways by which a semaphore signal can be operated from the output of an electronic circuit. The simplest method, only possible when the entire signal mechanism is very free-moving, is to provide a mechanical link between the mechanism (the counter-balance is a suitable part of it) and the armature of a low-voltage relay. The relay coil may then be connected to the output of a section bistable or EDOTIS unit. If the relay contacts are left in place, they may be used to operate other signals or in interlock systems. The relay may be replaced by a home-made solenoid consisting of a coil wound on such a former as a section of ballpoint refill using a steel pin as armature, but you will need some means, eg, a counterbalance weight, to return the signal arm when the coil is not energised. The coil will need a large number of turns, eg, 2,000, if it is to be operated by the output of a bistable or EDOTIS unit, ie, current in the region 10 to 50 mA.

The alternative method of driving a semaphore signal—and the only method of operating turnouts (formerly called points in the UK and switches in the USA)—is to use a turnout motor. This consists of a pair of solenoids enclosing a common armature, which is free to slide between them. Usual practice is to energise briefly one of the solenoids using ac or dc so that the armature is drawn into its core. It then remains in that position until the other solenoid is similarly energised, when it is drawn back again. A spigot on the armature provides for the mechanical link to the turnout blade or signal mechanism. Since only a brief burst of power (say ¼ second) is needed to operate the motor, current is normally switched using a passing-contact switch or an 'electric pencil'.

A turnout motor draws a substantial current. The dc resistance of each solenoid is typically about 5 Ω so that a 12 V dc supply could drive up to 2.4 A through it. Appreciable power is needed to draw a turnout blade against the spring. Semaphore signals for this kind of operation do not need to be so free moving! Obviously it is not possible to operate a turnout motor direct from the output of a section bistable or EDOTIS unit.

It is possible, however, to drive a turnout motor electronically and the driver circuit may itself be operated direct from a bistable or EDOTIS unit or from an ordinary two-way slide or toggle switch. A suitable circuit is shown in Figure 22.1.

How it works

One way of providing the burst of high current needed to operate a turnout motor is to charge or discharge a high-value capacitor through the solenoid winding. Suitable capacitors, however, would be both bulky and expensive. The alternative adopted in this circuit is to charge or discharge a smaller capacitor (32 μF) into the front end of an amplifier connected to the solenoid.

Turnout or signal setting is by single-pole changeover switch S1. When S1 is moved to the upper position in the figure, C1 charges via T1's base/emitter junction. The transistor conducts momentarily providing a bias for quasi-Darlington pair T3/T4, which also conducts momentarily sending a massive pulse of current through solenoid 1. The pulse lasts only a fraction of a second, but while S1 is left in position, capacitor C1 will be kept fully charged, ready to discharge when next the switch is operated.

When the switch is thrown to the lower position C1 discharges via T2's base/emitter junction. This transistor now conducts briefly providing bias for conventional Darlington pair T5/T6, which sends a pulse of power through solenoid 2. While the switch is in the lower position, capacitor C1 remains uncharged.

Construction

The circuit is suitable for tagstrip construction as it has only 10 components. The output transistors do not need heat sinks; they do not conduct for long enough to get hot.

Operation

The circuit *must* operate from a *smoothed* supply. Using an unsmoothed supply will, when S1 is in the upper position, cause C1 to charge via T1 then discharge via T2 with each pulse of supply energising *both* solenoids. There are several ways in which the circuit may be used. One unit may service a number of solenoid assemblies connected to the outputs via a two-pole rotary or push-button selector switch. Select the appropriate solenoid pair on the switch *and then operate switch S1*. If S1 is already 'up' and the 'up' position is required, you must operate 'down' then 'up', because no charge or discharge occurs until S1 is operated. Merely operating the selector switch will not energise any of the solenoids.

For the automatic operation of semaphore signals or turnouts one driver circuit will be needed for each turnout motor. Train-activated automatic turnout operation is rare, but perfectly feasible. The circuitry is, of course, the same as for a signal using this type of motor and is shown in Figure 22.2. One output transistor of the bistable or EDOTIS replaces switch S1. In Figure 22.2a when the bistable transistor Tb is off (ie, non-conductive) capacitor C1 charges via Rb and R1 so that solenoid 1 is energised. When this transistor becomes conductive, capacitor C1 discharges via R1 and Tb energising solenoid 2. Figure 22.2b shows the adaptation for EDOTIS circuits. When output A becomes live (ie, when a train enters the section) capacitor C1 charges via the EDOTIS output so solenoid 1 receives a pulse. When output A

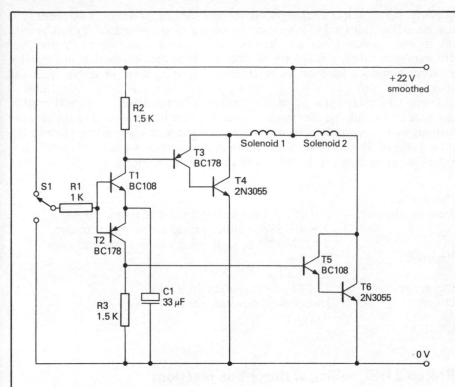

Figure 22.1 *Circuit of turnout motor driver.*

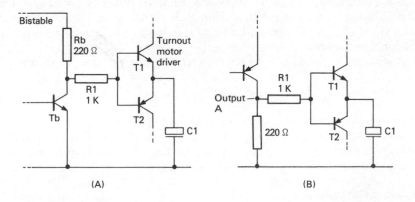

(A)   (B)

Figure 22.2 *Methods of driving the turnout motor driver from (a) a section bistable and (b) an EDOTIS unit.*

goes off, the capacitor discharges via R1 and the 220 Ω resistor, so solenoid 2 is energised. For this kind of operation involving bistables or EDOTIS units with the turnout motor driver all circuits must share a common earth line, but differences in supply voltage are immaterial. If a common earth is not feasible a relay should be used as an interface, the changeover contacts replacing switch S1.

There is a further application of the turnout motor driver. Switch S1 may be one pole of a multiple-pole two-way switch. If the driver is used to operate the turnout at a junction in a layout having an automatic signalling system, the other poles of S1 may be used as inputs to the junction signalling logic circuit. Signalling at junctions is the subject of the next two projects.

Parts needed

Semi-conductors:	2 × BC 108 or similar small-signal npn transistor.
	2 × BC 178 or similar small-signal pnp transistor.
	2 × 2N 3055 or similar high-power npn transistor.
Resistors:	1 × 1 K.
	2 × 1.5 K.
Capacitors:	1 × 32 μF electrolytic 24 V wkg.
Others:	Switches as required (see text).
	Turnout motor.

Project 23: Signalling at single-line junctions

So far the signalling systems described have concerned only section signalling intended on the prototype to prevent collisions between trains on the same line. Signalling at junctions is a little more complex—it must also take into account the setting of the turnouts (points or switches). Figure 23.1 shows a hypothetical single-line junction with two-aspect signalling. Imagine a train on section C approaching the junction. Signal Bu must not only protect the train against collision with any train in section B, but also against derailment if the turnout should be set for section E. The logic of signalling at junctions, then, may be summed up as:

Next section clear *and* turnouts set: green (or yellow or double yellow
                                                                    as appropriate)

Otherwise   : red

The detection of trains was considered in Projects 15 to 17; what is needed is a means of adding to this a facility for turning the signal red if the turnouts are set against the train. A manual over-ride was described in Project 18; this can be adapted to provide full junction signalling logic.

Two-aspect installation

For simplicity we shall assume that i) all the sections in Figure 24.1 are monitored using EDOTIS units; ii) the turnout is operated by the turnout motor driver circuit described in Project 22 or else that it is linked to a two-way switch; iii) the signals are all two-aspect types using bulbs.

Three signals, Bd, Bu and Bx, guard section B. Of these Bd is unaffected by the setting of the turnout—the aspect lit depends only on the occupancy of section B; it can therefore be driven straight from the EDOTIS outputs as described in Project 18.

Signals Bu and Bx, however, are affected by the setting of the turnout so an over-ride system must be used. This over-ride cannot be applied to the EDOTIS circuit itself, however, because this would affect signal Bd. So these signals must be driven by separate driver circuits having inputs from both the EDOTIS circuit and the turnout switch.

This signal driver circuit is the 'slave driver' which we have already met in connection with three-aspect signalling (Figure 19.3). Here it is used with minor modifications. The switch is ganged to the turnout switch and acts as an over-ride on the driver of whichever signal guards the unselected route. The complete circuitry (excluding the internal EDOTIS circuit) for signals Bd, Bu and Bx is shown in Figure 23.2.

Junction signal Cd poses a variety of complications. There are two sorts of junction colour-light signals. The older sort followed the practice for semaphore signals at junctions, having two separate heads, that for the main line being raised slightly above that for the branch. In effect it consists of two separate signals, one for each route, that for the route not selected being kept at red.

More recent installations use a single signal head with a route indicator. At a main-line/branch-line junction the route indicator normally consists of an array of five (occasionally three) white lights in an inclined straight line representing the direction of the branch. This is only illuminated *when the turnout is set for the branch and when the line is clear*. The signal itself, of course, shows whatever aspect is appropriate for the route selected.

Figure 23.3a shows the logic for signal Cd if the double-headed older-type installation is used. Each head needs its own driver circuit. Figure 23.3b shows the circuit for a single-headed signal with route indicator. In the latter circuit the 'A' outputs of both EDOTIS units are fed into the signal driver via R1/D1 and R2/D2, the unwanted output being short-circuited to ground via a pole of the turnout switch. Correct operation of the five-light indicator (those made by 'Eckon' use a single bulb and a light guide) is assured by using output B of the section E EDOTIS and including the turnout switch in the circuit.

The above examples and many to follow use further poles of the turnout switch. If only one pole is available, it may be used for an unlimited number of signalling circuits by either of the techniques shown in Figure 23.4. That in (b) is preferable but more expensive.

The other signals in Figure 23.1, namely Au, Cu, Dd, Eu and Fd, are not affected by the turnout and may be driven direct from the outputs of the relevant EDOTIS units.

Three-aspect installation

Without changing anything else, now let us assume that all the signals in Figure 23.1 are three-aspect types. More signals will be affected by the turnout than in the two-aspect installation, because signals Bd, Cu and Eu now include the junction in their 'scope'.

Signals Bu and Bx will now be affected by i) the setting of the turnout, ii) the occupancy of section B and iii) the occupancy of section A. The circuit for the red aspect is the same as in the two-aspect installation; one side of both green

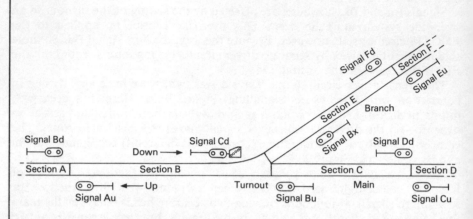

Figure 23.1 *Position of signals in part of a hypothetical junction layout with two-aspect signalling.*

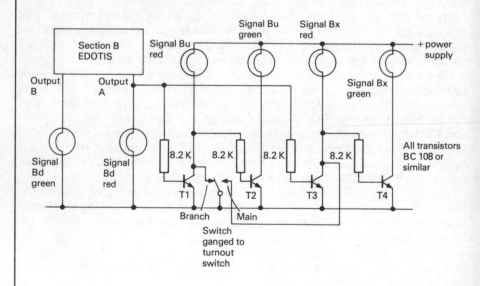

Figure 23.2 *Circuit for driving signals Bd, Bu and Bx in Figure 23.1.*

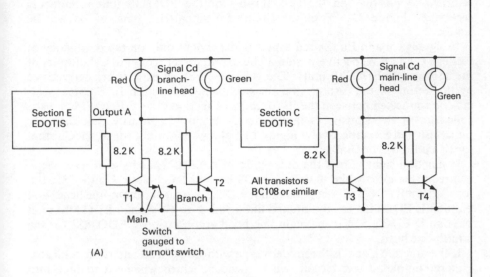

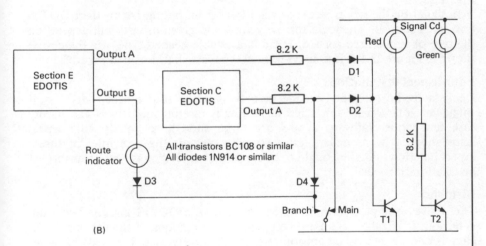

Figure 23.3 *Circuit for driving junction signal Cd in Figure 23.1 if (A) it is a double-headed type and (B) it is a single-headed type with route indicator.*

and yellow aspects is wired to T2 in the signal driver; the other sides are returned to positive via the two outputs of the EDOTIS unit monitoring section A. Figure 23.5 gives the circuit for signal Bu; that for Bx will be similar.

In signals Cu and Eu the red aspect is dependent only on the occupancy of sections C and E respectively, so may be driven direct from the 'A' outputs of the appropriate EDOTIS units. The yellow and green aspects are determined by the setting of the turnout and the occupancy of section B. These aspects may be connected between the 'B' outputs of section C or E EDOTIS and the collectors of the transistors in the driver circuits previously described for signals Bu and Bx respectively. Figure 23.6 shows the circuit for signal Cu; that for signal Eu will be similar.

If junction signal Cd is the older type of double-headed signal, each head will require a circuit like that for signals Bu and Bx. Follow Figure 23.5 but for 'Section B EDOTIS' read 'Section C EDOTIS' (for the main-line head) and 'Section E EDOTIS' for the branch-line head. For 'Section A EDOTIS' read 'Section D EDOTIS' for the main-line head and 'Section F EDOTIS' for the branch-line head.

If the junction signal is the modern type with single head and route indicator a more complex driver circuit will be needed, which will need to take into account the outputs of no fewer than four EDOTIS units. This is shown in Figure 23.7.

In signal Bd the red aspect is driven direct from output 'A' of the EDOTIS unit for section B. The logic for the yellow and green aspects will depend on the type of signal used for Cd. If Cd is a double-headed type, use the circuit shown in Figure 23.8a. If a single-headed type, use that shown in Figure 23.8b.

Four-aspect installations

Deliberately no attempt is made here to describe four-aspect signalling at single-line junctions. Four-aspect signalling is rare on single lines and in any case few model railway layouts are large enough to justify four-aspect installations. The modeller, however, who masters the principles of three-aspect junction signalling ought to be capable of extending them to four-aspect installations if needed.

Bistables

The above examples have assumed the use of EDOTIS circuits for train detection. If bistables are used, complementary versions of the various driver circuits can be devised as appropriate. Alternatively, use 'inverted' bistables with pnp transistors; the driver circuits described in this chapter can then be used without modification.

LEDs

If the two-aspect installation is modelled using signals with LEDs instead of bulbs, simply replace the bulbs by resistors and 'string' the signals between the output transistor collectors (Project 21). Three- and four-aspect signals with LEDs use the same circuits as bulb signals with suitable series resistors (see Project 19 and 20).

Semaphore signals

Each signal (ie, each arm) must be driven by a relay connected to an EDOTIS unit or by a turnout motor and driver (Project 23). Junction signals must be regarded as two separate signals and will require a logic circuit as in Figure 23.2. Three-aspect signals are replaced by combined home-and-distant types, which must also be regarded as two separate signals. Fully automatic semaphore signalling systems may be constructed by modellers having the necessary resources—and patience!

Parts needed
See text.

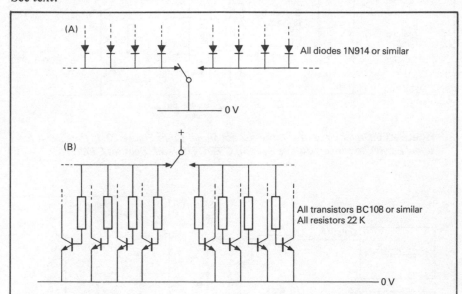

Figure 23.4 *Two ways of providing multiple switching for signalling logic from a single-pole two-way switch.*

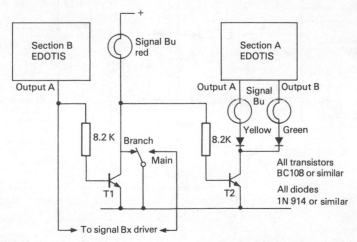

Figure 23.5 *Driver circuit for three-aspect signal Bu in Figure 23.1. The driver for signal Bx would be similar.*

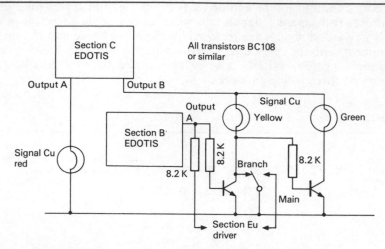

Figure 23.6 *Driver circuit for three-aspect signal Cu in Figure 23.1; the circuit for signal Eu will be similar, but for Section C EDOTIS read 'Section E EDOTIS'.*

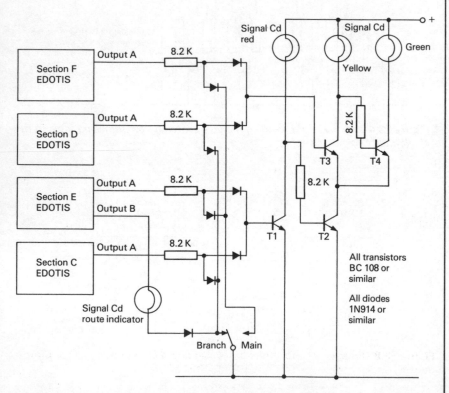

Figure 23.7 *Driver circuit for three-aspect signal Cd in Figure 23.1 if a single-headed type with a route indicator.*

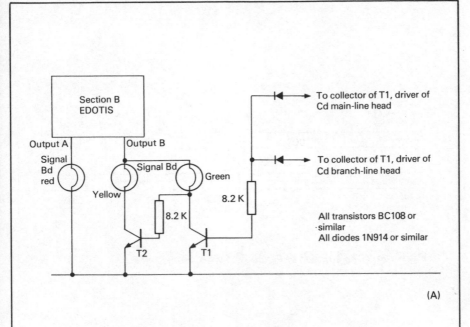

To collector of T1, driver of
Cd main-line head

To collector of T1, driver of
Cd branch-line head

All transistors BC108 or
·similar
All diodes 1N914 or similar

(A)

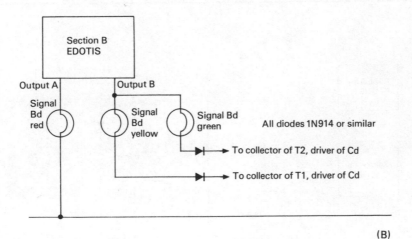

All diodes 1N914 or similar

To collector of T2, driver of Cd

To collector of T1, driver of Cd

(B)

Figure 23.8 *Driver circuits for three-aspect signal Bd in Figure 23.1 (A) if Cd is a double-headed type and (B) if Cd is a single-headed type.*

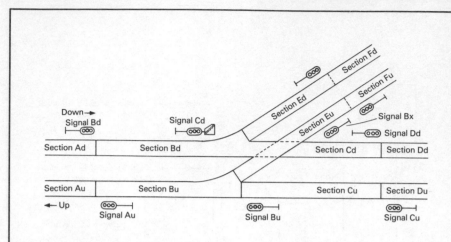

Figure 24.1 *The junction of Figure 23.1 with double track.*

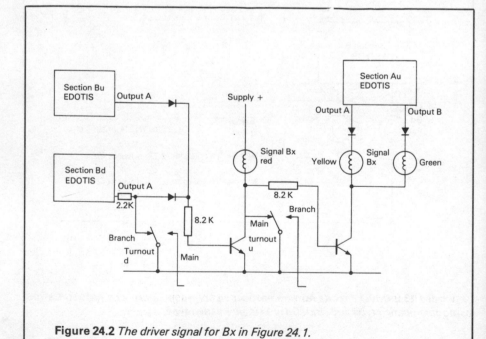

Figure 24.2 *The driver signal for Bx in Figure 24.1.*

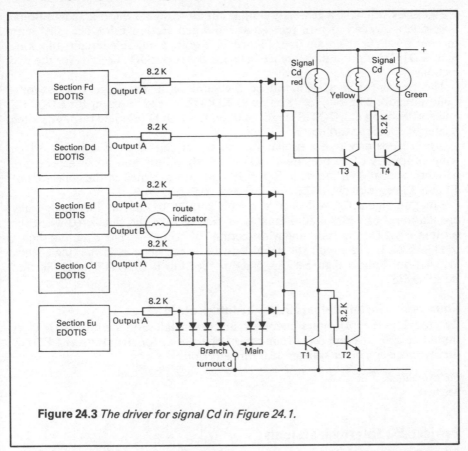

Figure 24.3 *The driver for signal Cd in Figure 24.1.*

Project 24: Signalling at double-line junctions

Figure 24.1 shows the layout of Figure 23.1 but with double track throughout. Section names have been retained, but are designated u or d for up or down. Similarly signal names are unchanged; despite the doubling of the line the number of signals is the same. The principal difference between the logic for this installation and its single-line counterpart is the complication caused by the diamond crossing. For train detection purposes it is best to include the diamond crossing in Bd and Eu.

As a consequence of the diamond crossing, signal Cd cannot be cleared for the main line if section Eu is occupied; similarly signal Bx cannot be cleared if section Bd is occupied with turnout d set for the main line. So the logic for these two signals must incorporate additional over-rides.

For ease of comparison with the single-line installation, the following assumes the use of EDOTIS on all sections, three-aspect colour-light signalling using bulbs and a single-headed signal Cd with route indicator.

The circuit for signal Bu is identical to that in the single-line system. Follow Figure 23.5 but for 'Section A EDOTIS' read 'Section Au EDOTIS' and for 'Section B EDOTIS' read 'Section Bu EDOTIS'. The turnout switch relates of course to turnout u.

Signal Bx will have a generally similar circuit to signal Bu, but an additional over-ride is needed to turn the signal red when section Bd is occupied with turnout d set for the main line. Figure 24.2 gives a suitable circuit. Blocking diodes D1/D2 prevent interference between the two EDOTIS units for the two sections B.

The circuit for signal Cu will be the same as in the single-track layout. Follow Figure 23.6 but for 'Section B EDOTIS' read 'Section Bu EDOTIS' and for 'Section C EDOTIS' read 'Section Cu EDOTIS'. The turnout switch relates of course to turnout u.

Signal Eu is driven in a similar way to signal Cu. The red aspect is driven from output A of section Eu EDOTIS. Both yellow and green aspects are wired to output B of the same EDOTIS unit and returned to the collectors of T1 and T2 respectively of the circuit shown in Figure 24.2.

Junction signal Cd will need a circuit similar to that in the single-track installation, but with an additional over-ride to turn the signal red when the turnout is set for the main line with section Eu occupied. The circuit is shown in Figure 24.3. The circuit for signal Bd will be the same as in the single-track installation. Follow Figure 23.8b, but for 'Section B EDOTIS' read 'Section Bd EDOTIS'.

Four-aspect installations, LEDs, bistables etc.

By studying the principles involved in the installation described, readers should be able to adapt it for four-aspect operation, for signals using LEDs or for layouts using other systems of train detection.

Parts needed
See text.

Project 25: Interlock systems

An interlock system (for the purposes of this book) is one which automatically stops a train at a red signal and restarts it when the signal clears. Their use on complex layouts can be most effective, since by making collisions almost impossible large numbers of trains can operate automatically. Interlock systems are of two sorts: active and passive. In an *active* system the controller itself is automatically adjusted first to stop and later to restart the train. In a *passive* system the controller is unaffected, the supply between controller and train being interrupted when the train is to stop and restored when the train is to restart. Obviously active interlock systems give more realistic operation, but are correspondingly more complicated.

Active interlock

You need a controller with a voltage control system (Projects 13 and 14). You must, of course, have an automatic signalling system (Projects 18 to 24) which presupposes the use of a train detection system (Projects 15 to 17). An additional train detector will be needed a suitable distance ahead of the signal to be interlocked. A magnet/reed switch system (Project 15) is recommended as this alone is electrically isolated from the track; moreover it is only tripped by locomotives or other vehicles which have been deliberately modified by the fitting of a magnet. Other systems which are liable to be tripped by vehicles further down the train would pose special problems when the train has restarted and its front portion has passed the signal turning it red!

Figure 25.1 shows a typical active interlock circuit. Under normal conditions, ie, when the signal being interlocked is clear, T1 and T2 are both without bias; since this blocks both bias paths for T4, the bistable T3/T4 is normally locked with T3 'on', although it cannot conduct because T2 blocks its collector circuit. As T4 is locked 'off', T5 receives no bias and being non-conductive has no effect on the controller. So trains continue to run normally; activating the reed switch has no effect. When the signal is red, T1 and T2 receive bias and conduct. T3 continues to receive bias and is now able to conduct, but T4 and T5 still receive no bias, so the bistable remains in its original state. There is still no effect on the controller.

If, while the signal is red, reed switch RS1 is activated by a train approaching the signal, T4 receives bias and the bistable changes state. (Optional LED D1 lights up indicating that the interlock is operating; this LED is useful as it explains why the train has stopped if the signal aspect is out of sight of the operator.) T5 now receives bias and cuts off T6 so that control voltage capacitor C1 discharges at the rate set by brake control VR3 bringing the train to a gradual halt. The train will now remain stopped until the signal clears. When this happens, the removal of bias from T1, T2 and T4 forces the bistable back into its original state. T5 loses its bias, T6 conducts again and the control voltage capacitor recharges at the rate set by inertia control VR2, causing the train to start again gently.

The system as described must share the controller's power supply and have common earth with the train detection circuitry. The former poses no problems. The latter may do and certainly will if EDOTIS is the train detection/signalling system. If used with EDOTIS, introduce a relay or opto-isolator between the train detector and interlock input. Construction is straightforward; Veroboard or similar is recommended.

Passive interlock

Although passive interlocks are far simpler than active ones, they nevertheless pose serious problems, the biggest of which is that the controller output has to be switched. To do this using semi-conductors would be both expensive (because the current is bi-directional a complementary pair of power transistors would be needed) and inefficient (since voltage loss would inevitably occur). For these reasons a relay is preferable.

The system shown in Figure 25.2 is especially suitable for use with EDOTIS, since the block sections are already isolated. No additional train detection is needed, but a new rail break ahead of the interlocked signal isolates that portion of line. The feed to this portion is taken from the feed to the rest of the section via relay contacts, the relay coil being driven from either output of the next section's EDOTIS unit. When that section is occupied (and the signal is red), the relay contacts *open*, cutting off power from the interlocked portion. Any train entering this portion of line while the signal is red will stop dead before the signal. (Ingenious readers may like to adapt the capacitor slow-down from Project 3 for use with this circuit.) Connecting a resistor (1 K is suitable) across the relay contacts will ensure that stopped trains in the interlocked portion are still detected by the section's EDOTIS unit. When the

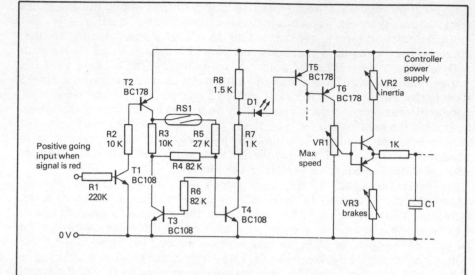

Figure 25.1 *Active interlock circuit. Part of the controller circuit is shown as well.*

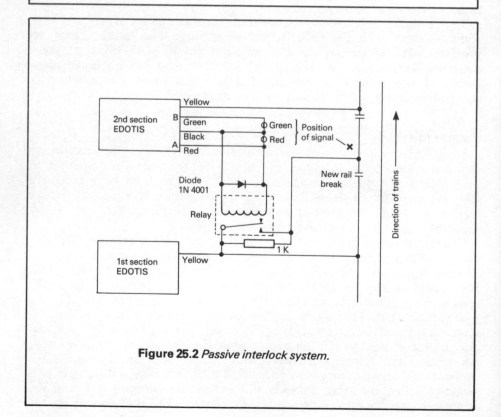

Figure 25.2 *Passive interlock system.*

signal clears, the relay coil is de-energised and the stopped train restarts (abruptly).

The system is crude, but simple and effective. It can easily be combined with a semaphore signalling system, the relay armature driving the signal mechanism. It can be adapted for use with other train detection systems besides EDOTIS, provided the interlock portion is isolated at both ends.

Parts needed
i) Active interlock (as far as T6)

Semi-conductors:	3 × BC 108 or similar.
	3 × BC 178 or similar.
	1 × LED, size and colour to suit construction.
Resistors:	1 × 1 K.
	1 × 1.5 K.
	2 × 10 K.
	1 × 27 K.
	2 × 82 K.
	1 × 220 K.
Miscellaneous:	Veroboard, reed switch.

ii) Passive interlock
Relay.
1 K resistor.
EDOTIS units.

Project 26: Searchlight signals using multicolour LEDs

Most model searchlight signals use two or three bulbs in a massive signal base, the light being fed to the lens via a light pipe. This kind of model has several disadvantages. Firstly, the massive base can cause mounting difficulties. Secondly, the light transmission system tends to make the colours feeble. Thirdly, gantry-mounted or multiple-head signals are very difficult to model.

The latest generation of multicolour LEDs, however, has made it possible to construct 4 mm and 7 mm scale searchlight signals with deep, realistic colour generated prototypically within the signal head itself. This eliminates the mounting difficulties and makes it possible to construct gantry-, bracket-, post- and ground-mounted signals and even multiple-head types, such as the former GWR home-and-distant types, the LMS Mirfield experimental speed signalling installations or the junction signals on the LMR Camden to Watford dc line.

The heart of the signal head is a device available from Maplin Electronic Supplies Ltd (catalogue number YY61R) which incorporates in one colourless encapsulation red and green LED light sources. There are two important differences between this and certain other multicolour LED light sources on the market. Firstly, the colours obtained from this device are a very deep red, a bright green and a bright amber/yellow whose exact tint can be adjusted. Some other devices give a pale pink and a pale yellowish-green, which make unconvincing signals. Secondly, this device has three leads: green cathode, red cathode and common anode. This makes it far easier to use than many other types, which have only two leads and with which you have to use ac to get yellow.

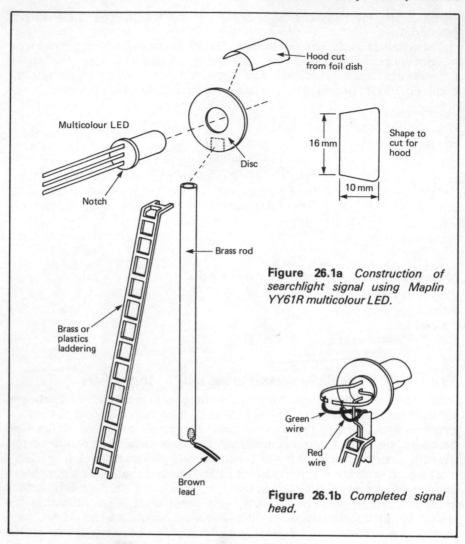

Figure 26.1a *Construction of searchlight signal using Maplin YY61R multicolour LED.*

Figure 26.1b *Completed signal head.*

The one problem with this device is its size: its body is 5 mm in diameter and about 10 mm long. However, although this means that the bulk of its body inevitably protrudes out of the front of the signal head (as do the bulbs in many multi-lens signal models), it is effectively hidden beneath the hood and, being made of 'water clear' epoxy resin, it just vanishes into the background, even when the signal is alight. As on the prototype, to see the aspect clearly the signal must be observed from a position more or less directly in front.

Construction of the signal

As with the simple signal described in Project 4, the leads of the LED are used for both electrical and scenic functions, so a construction method will be described. The other parts needed for the post-mounted version are as follows. For the post you will need a length of brass tube—suitable sizes are 48 mm long × ⅛ in (3 mm) diameter for 4 mm scale and 80 mm long × $\frac{3}{16}$ in (5 mm) diameter for 7 mm scale. The disc, which may be of plastic or metal, should be 10 to 12 mm diameter for 4 mm scale or 16 to 20 mm diameter for 7 mm scale; in either case the central hole needs to be 5 mm diameter. There is a standard washer of suitable dimensions for 4 mm scale, which saves a lot of work. Also needed is brass or plastic laddering, fine sleeved wire in red, green and brown and some material from which to fashion the hood—an old foil dish (the sort of thing ready-baked pies come in) is ideal.

Solder or glue the post to the disc, ensuring that it is straight, and leaving 2 mm clearance between the edge of the hole and the top of the post. Insert the LED through the hole and turn it so that the notch in the rim is adjacent to the top of the post. *Carefully* bend down the lowest lead of the LED (the one adjacent to the notch) so that it contacts the post and solder it to the post—do not bend any of the leads of the LED too close to its body or you may damage the device. Solder a brown sleeved wire to the base of the post; this gives us the common anode connection. Solder or glue a suitable length of ladder to the top of the post.

Now for the trickiest part. Thread suitable lengths of red and green sleeved wire up through the post and pull them out from beneath the LED—you will need fine forceps to do this. (You can't do this earlier in construction because the soldering to the post would melt the sleeving, causing short circuits.) Pull out about an inch (25 mm) of sleeved wire or each colour at the top of the post. Carefully bend round the two remaining leads of the LED to form a safety hoop as shown in Figure 26.1, but do not let them actually touch. Bend the sleeved wires outward and upward to simulate supports for the safety hoop and solder them near to the ends of the LED leads; the red wire goes to the central lead of the LED, which is the red cathode, and the green wire goes to the top lead, which is the green cathode. Cut out a suitably shaped piece of foil for the hood, roll it into shape and glue it on top of the LED body which protrudes out of the front of the disc. The hood should be sized so as to just cover the LED.

Paint the hood and front of the disc matt black; the rest of the signal should be matt pale grey. In 4 mm scale the signal head may well be slightly over-scale, but when painted this is hardly noticeable. What does look good is the remarkably slim back to the signal head, which will fascinate spectators not used to LED technology. The signal can be superdetailed by adding track circuit diamond signs, number plates, telephone boxes etc to the taste of the constructor.

Operation

If you followed the instructions above, your completed signal has three wires issuing from the foot of the post: red, which is the cathode of the red light source; green, which is the cathode of the green light source; and brown, which is the common anode connection. Although there are only three wires, the signal is capable of displaying three aspects: red, green and yellow.

The two light sources in the multicolour LED resemble ordinary single-colour LEDs electrically and all the normal LED precautions must be taken—for example, do not apply reverse voltages, and always include a series resistor to limit the current to a maximum of 20 mA. In fact the red source is much brighter than the green source and for this reason it is recommended that separate series resistors be used in the cathode circuits of each junction, so that the current ratios can be adjusted to give a more consistent brightness between the different aspects. For example, the red cathode resistor may be 1 K and the green 470 Ω. There is a second reason for this—the yellow aspect is obtained by putting on both light sources together. The exact tint of the yellow depends upon the proportions of red and green light being generated within the device. A good prototypical 'signal yellow' is often obtained when the green current is roughly twice the red current, ie, the green cathode resistor is half the red cathode resistor. The tint can be adjusted by changing the values of these resistors—lower the red cathode resistor to make the yellow more reddish; increase it to make the yellow more greenish.

Figure 26.2 *Circuit to enable searchlight signal to be operated from EDOTIS units.*

Type of signal	Input 1	Input 2	Input 3
2-aspect 'home' or 'stop'	EDOTIS 1 A	not used	EDOTIS 1 B
2-aspect 'distant'	EDOTIS 1 A	not used	Supply +
3-aspect	EDOTIS 1 A	EDOTIS 2 A	EDOTIS 1 B

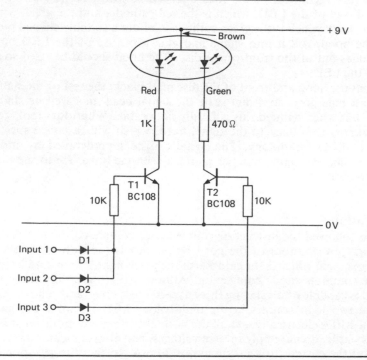

The signal can be used manually or automatically. For manual two-aspect operation as a 'home' or 'stop' signal use a single-pole double-throw switch to select which of the two cathode circuits is connected to the supply negative. For a distant signal leave the green cathode circuit permanently connected and use a single-pole single-throw switch to switch on the red source when the yellow aspect is required. For three-aspect manual operation, use two separate switches corresponding to first-section occupation and second-section occupation. The first switch circuit is as for a two-aspect home signal; the second switch is as for the distant signal.

For automatic operation the switches in the manual circuits may be replaced by the npn transistors in section bistables, the cathode resistors becoming the collector load resistors. For a three-aspect signal, blocking diodes (1N914 or similar) will be needed between the 'red' cathode resistor and the two 'on when occupied' transistor collectors—these are essential to prevent mutual interference between the two bistables.

Because EDOTIS as described in Project 18 has positive-going outputs and because the LED in the signal has a common anode, there are difficulties in driving the signal direct from EDOTIS outputs. It is simpler either to devise a track circuiting system with npn output transistors or to use a separate signal driver circuit as shown in Figure 26.2. For some applications not all the components may be needed.

Parts needed
i) Signal
See text. Current limiting resistors.
ii) Signal drive circuit (Figure 26.2)
2 × npn small-signal transistor (BC108 or similar).
3 × small-signal diode (1N914 or similar).
2 × 10 K resistor.

Part 6

Locomotive and coach lighting

Preamble

That the romance of railways is enhanced by the night is evidenced in the work of many railway artists. On main lines traffic continues through the night and includes types of train rarely seen in daytime, such as sleeping-car expresses, mail trains and maintenance trains. In the dark, signal lamps, train headlamps and coach lighting become more conspicuous, adding extra drama to the atmosphere.

Many railway modellers enjoy simulating night-time scenes. Station lights, street lighting and lights in lineside buildings are scenic and electrical matters outside the scope of this book, but train lighting is a different matter. Effective constant-brightness headlights, tail lights and coach lighting can only be achieved using electronic circuitry, all of which, compared with many of the earlier projects, are surprisingly simple. The high-frequency generator for coach lighting, for instance, uses only 13 components (apart from those in its power supply), none of which is expensive.

If you have not tried night-scene modelling, you have missed a thoroughly worthwhile railway modelling experience. If your scenic capabilities—like the author's—are weak, the dark will conceal a multitude of sins of omission and commission. In addition, the sight of a fully lit model express train thundering past an illuminated signal and disappearing into the dark, its tail lamp gradually fading into the distance, gives a thrill that words cannot describe.

Project 27: Head and tail lamps using LEDs

Some proprietary model locomotives are fitted with headlamps or route indicators which light up when the train is running; these employ miniature 12 V bulbs connected in parallel with the motor. Sometimes the illumination is directionally controlled, eg, the headlamps only light when the loco is running forward or, on a double-ended diesel-outline model only the headboard at the end that is facing forwards is illuminated. Similarly some proprietary guard's vans have a red tail lamp that only lights up when the train is running forwards. Directional control is obtained by including a suitable diode in series with the lamp(s).

Effective though such lighting is, it has two drawbacks. Firstly, the lighting

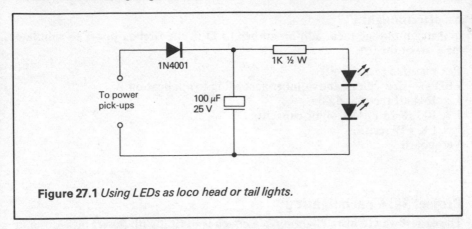

Figure 27.1 *Using LEDs as loco head or tail lights.*

is extinguished altogether when the controller is at zero. Secondly, the brightness varies with the setting of the controller. Both problems can be mitigated to some extent by the simple LED system described below, although the lights will, of course, be extinguished when the controller is off or at 'stop'. A system for running headlamps and tail lamps quite independently of the controller is described in Project 28.

How it works

The brightness of LED illumination is much less dependent on supply voltage than that of tungsten lamps. So if a headlamp assembly consisting of a diode (for directional control) and two miniature lamp bulbs were replaced by the circuit shown in Figure 27.1 *omitting for the time being capacitor C1*, one result should be improved consistency of brightness. Yellow LEDs are a fair substitute for the colour of old-style oil-burning train headlamps.

If, however, you use a PWM controller, you can go a stage better. Since each pulse is theoretically a pulse of *full power*, you can use a capacitor to store that power, acting as a 'reservoir' to keep the LEDs at constant brightness. The result is very effective, giving headlamps (or tail lamps if you use red LEDs) whose brightness is apparently constant at all settings of the controller, except, of course, at zero. But you may find that just above zero there is a setting on your controller where the pulses are too brief to set (or keep) the train moving, but where nevertheless there is sufficient power to light the lights. By skilful manipulation of the speed control, then, you may be able to achieve constant-brightness lighting, even with the train stopped.

The presence of diode D1 means that these headlights and tail lamps will be directionally controlled—be sure to connect the circuit to the power pick-ups the right way round! The diode also protects the LED(s) against inverse voltages. If you wish to run your train with your lights off, you will need to include a switch in series with D1.

Construction

The circuit is simple and the components small. Mounted on a small piece of Veroboard or similar, it should be possible to miniaturise the circuit sufficiently to fit in the smallest 00/H0 gauge locos.

An afterthought

In a steam-outline loco, add an amber LED in the firebox doors to simulate the glow of the fire.

Parts needed (per circuit)
LED(s)—size, colour and number according to application.
1 × 1N4001 rectifier diode.
1 × 100 μF 25 V electrolytic capacitor.
1 × 1 K $\frac{1}{2}$ W resistor.
Veroboard.

Project 28: Coach lighting

The easiest way to install lighting in a coach is to fit it with power pick-ups and from these drive one or more miniature 12 V lamp bulbs strategically located inside the coach. The brightness of the lighting will, of course, depend on the controller setting and the lights will be extinguished when the controller is turned to 'stop'. Moreover, unless a switch is fitted somewhere on the coach, the train cannot be run with the lights off.

With a multiple-train-control-type controller where the track is permanently live, constant-brightness coach lighting is possible. But again, a switch on the coach or an accessory control unit responding to the controller will be needed if the train is to be run with the lights off. An ideal coach lighting system should be capable of operating quite independently of the controller, of giving constant brightness, of being switched on and off from the operator's control panel and of installation with minimal modification to existing electrical facilities. The ideal is probably unattainable, but the system described here is a good approach to it and is simple and inexpensive. It uses sub-miniature tungsten bulbs; one day it may be possible to use LEDs for coach lighting, but at the time of writing LEDs are not bright enough and cannot give white light—yellow LEDs are a poor approximation to tungsten lamps.

The principle

A generating circuit injects high-frequency (hf) alternating current (ac) into the track via the same wires as the power from the controller. This ac is the power for the coach lighting. Since capacitors conduct ac but not dc, these are used both at the output of the hf generator and at the input to the coach lights to prevent the dc from the controller interfering with the lighting system. (Actually a very feeble glow may be seen from the coach lights when the hf generator is off and the train is running slowly under pulsed control. This is because at the end of each pulse from the controller the locomotive motor generates a pulse of inductive overshoot. These pulses are of opposite polarity and therefore behave as ac, passing through the capacitors and lighting the lamps. The glow is so feeble that it is barely visible even in the dark.)

A suitable hf generator circuit is shown in Figure 28.1. It consists of a multivibrator (T1 and T2) which generates ac at a frequency of about 30 KHz, ie, 30,000 cycles per second. T3 amplifies its output and drives the complementary-symmetrical output pair T4/T5, which delivers the output to the track via capacitor C3.

There are three reasons for the use of such a high frequency, as opposed to, say, the 100 Hz used for the PWM controllers in Projects 9, 10 and 14. Firstly, low-frequency ac would interfere with the running of locomotives, especially when PWM controllers are used. Secondly, lower frequencies set the armatures of loco motors vibrating, giving an objectionable noise. However, 30 KHz is outside the audible spectrum of sound and therefore silent. Thirdly, the resistance of capacitors to ac (known as their *reactance*) falls as the frequency of the ac rises. At 30 KHz 1 μF corresponds to 5.3 Ω so small and inexpensive mica and polyester capacitors can be used for coupling; at lower frequencies ac electrolytic types would be needed; these are bulky and expensive.

How it works

The multivibrator (T1 and T2 in Figure 28.1) resembles the symmetrical bistable that we met in Project 14, but the coupling between the two transistors is via capacitors. As in the bistable, as one transistor conducts it cuts the other one off—but only for as long as it takes for the coupling capacitor to charge up. When this happens the transistors automatically reverse their roles. So in the multivibrator the transistors repeatedly change from one state to the other at a frequency fixed by the values of the coupling capacitors (C1, C2), bias resistors (R2, R3) and supply voltage. The voltage on either collector will alternate between near zero when the transistor is 'on' and near supply voltage when the transistor is 'off'. This output is amplified and applied to a capacitor (C3) whose charge and discharge currents form an ac power output.

Strictly a 24 V dc smoothed power supply is needed for the 12 V ac output necessary for full brightness; lower supply voltages give lower output and dimmer lighting; 18 V is probably the lower limit of acceptability. 'Grain-of-wheat' 12 V bulbs are the traditional type used in coach lighting, but the author prefers the slightly larger bulbs used in slot racing cars which are cheaper and far brighter. Consumption is about 20 to 30 mA per bulb and the hf generator should drive 12 or more.

The bulbs

Installing the bulbs is a constructional rather than an electronic matter and therefore strictly beyond the scope of this book. As many power pick-ups as possible should be used to ensure continuity over turnouts, crossovers, 'dead' sections (if used) and dirty or twisted tracks. If a train of permanently coupled stock is being lit, it is worthwhile fitting wires between coaches so that all lights receive power from all pick-ups. It is recommended that each bulb have a 0.33 μF or 0.47 μF capacitor fitted in series. Without this the lamp will also be lit by the controller output and the facility will be lost for running trains with the lights off. All conventionally fitted loco headlamps (with or without direction-sensing diodes) will be lit by the hf system as well as by the controller.

Lighting LEDs from the hf system

LEDs for loco headlamps or for loco, guard's van or brake end tail lamps can also be driven from the hf supply, if required, but they will not be directionally controlled as they were in Project 27; they will light up whenever the hf generator (and therefore the coach lighting) is working. To ensure isolation from the controller's dc output, capacitor coupling is recommended; Figure 28.2 suggests circuits for twin-LED and single-LED applications. No current-limiting resistor is needed in the twin-LED application; the capacitor itself limits the current, 0.01 μF (corresponding to 530 Ω at 30 KHz) being a suitable value for most applications.

Use of the hf generator in connection with other equipment

The output coupling capacitor C3 in Figure 28.1 prevents dc or pulsed dc from the controller from entering the hf generator and interfering with it directly. Certain types of controller, eg, the PWM type described in Project 14, when delivering full power, effectively short-circuit the coach lighting, turning it out and causing very heavy current consumption on the part of the hf generator. The output of the hf generator, while unable to interfere with locomotives directly, can affect the function of controllers having a feedback loop, into which the ac penetrates.

Both difficulties can be eliminated by fitting a 2.7 mH (milliHenry) choke in series with the output of the controller. This is a coil which presents a low resistance to the dc output from the controller (if possible use one having a dc resistance no greater than 2 Ω), but which has an effective resistance of 500 Ω at 30 KHz. This, then, prevents the controller from short circuiting the power for the lighting. The further addition of a 0.1 μF capacitor across the output terminals of the controller will prevent ac from the hf generator from entering the controller's feedback loop.

The hf lighting system may be used in conjunction with EDOTIS units. The hf generator acts as a second controller, the ac feed to an illuminated train activating the current detector in the normal way. So, while the hf units is on, an EDOTIS unit will detect a rake of illuminated coaches even in the absence of a locomotive, but if the hf unit is switched off, the 'occupied' indication will persist only as long as it takes for the auxiliary current to charge the coupling capacitors in the train lighting.

A final word of warning. The hf generator may interfere with other domestic electrical equipment. It is a very effective transmitter of radio interference. While it is unlikely to upset reception of local radio and TV transmissions seriously it may affect reception of distant radio stations in the medium- and long-wave broadcast bands. Be considerate in your use of this circuit.

Parts needed

Hf generator: 3 × BC 108 or similar small-signal npn transistor.
 1 × BC 337.
 1 × BC 327.
 1 × 680 Ω resistor.
 2 × 8.2 K resistor.
 2 × 33 K resistor.
 2 × 0.01 μF capacitor.
 1 × 1 μF non-polarised capacitor.
 1 × 18 V to 24 V smoothed dc power supply.

Lighting: Miniature 12 V bulbs.
 0.33 or 0.47 μF capacitor, one for each bulb.

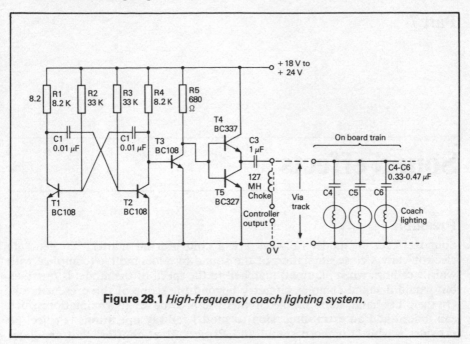

Figure 28.1 *High-frequency coach lighting system.*

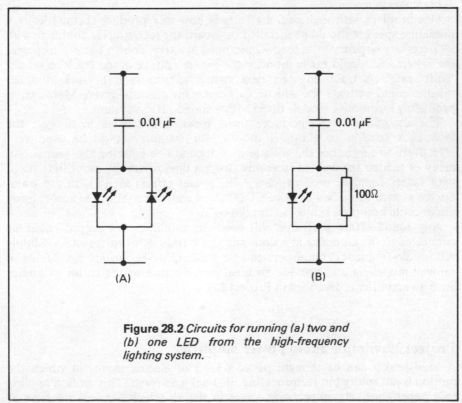

Figure 28.2 *Circuits for running (a) two and (b) one LED from the high-frequency lighting system.*

Part 7

Sound effects

Preamble

Sound effects on model railways are a controversial matter. To generate electronically a close simulation of the sound of a locomotive (complete with whistle or horn when required) matched to the speed of the model is *possible*, but would demand complex circuitry beyond the scope of the present book. On the other hand, quite simple circuits will provide an approximation which can indeed add an extra dimension to model railway operations. Project 30 provides a whistle or horn sound and Project 31 a 'chuffer' that simulates exhaust steam sound.

One problem with such sound effects is how to reproduce them. Ideally a miniature speaker should be installed on-board the locomotive, complete with all necessary circuitry. The loco would need to carry its own battery to power the system, but could easily monitor the power voltage in the track to set the 'chuff rate'. A train-mounted reed switch passing over a track-mounted magnet could activate the whistle or horn. One manufacturer, Mainline, is producing locomotive models fitted with a sound-effects system.

The alternative is one or more fixed speakers concealed in or near the layout. A speaker in a tunnel mouth, for instance, could be used very effectively to reproduce the whistle of a locomotive entering the tunnel. An array of hidden speakers at intervals along a line, driven by amplifiers fitted with faders could be used to 'carry' the sound effects along with the train. Such a system could be linked to EDOTIS or section bistables. Model railway audio could become a subject in its own right.

Any sound effect generator will need an amplifier. Its output could be connected to the amplifier in a domestic radio receiver or hi-fi system. Simple AF (audio-frequency) amplifiers can be made quite easily, are invaluable in railway modelling and provide an ideal introduction to the realm of audio. Such an amplifier is described in Project 29.

Project 29: Simple audio power amplifier

A loudspeaker can be thought of as a kind of electric motor in which the motion is not rotary but reciprocating, ie, back and forth. This motion applied to a paper cone sets up pressure waves in the air which our ears perceive as 'sound'. The quality of the sound is determined by its frequency (pitch), amplitude (strength) and rate of rise or fall of amplitude. The electrical input to the speaker needed to produce 'meaningful' sound, then, will consist of ac (alternating current) of varying frequency and amplitude. The range of audible frequencies extends from about 20 Hz to about 16,000 Hz.

In most of the projects in the earlier parts of this book transistors are employed as switches only. In these applications a transistor may be 'off', ie, not conducting so that its collector voltage approaches the supply voltage, or it may be 'on', ie, conducting flat out so that its collector voltage approaches zero. This kind of operation is not normally suitable for audio applications, because the transistor cannot respond to an ac input. For instance, an npn transistor that is 'off' can respond to a positive-going input by becoming conductive, but cannot respond to a negative-going input because it cannot go any further 'off'.

If, however, we bias the transistor so that it is 'half-way on', a positive-going input will increase collector current (resulting in a fall in collector voltage) while a negative-going input will cause a diminution in collector current (resulting in a rise in collector voltage). In designing AF (audio-frequency) amplifier stages care must be taken to bias the transistors so that the output voltage is free to rise or fall with varying input signal. It is wise to arrange for the quiescent (ie, no-input) output voltage to be approximately half the supply voltage, especially in the later stages of an amplifier. In the output stage any deviation of the quiescent output voltage from Vcc/2 (ie, half the supply voltage) would severely restrict the level of output available.

A practical 1 Watt amplifier

Figure 29.1 gives the circuit for an amplifier that is capable of running from a 9 V supply and delivering about 1 W into a 3 Ω to 8 Ω speaker. Voltage gain is 10 and input impedance about 50 K. One of the advantages of an AF signal being ac is that it will pass through capacitors, which isolate dc. So C1 at the input admits AF signals but prevents any dc from the signal source from upsetting the biasing of T1; this is set by R1/R2/R3. The potential divider R1/R2 sets the base voltage on T1 at about 1.1 V (upon which the AF input is superimposed). This 1.1 V puts about 0.4 V across R3 which sets the collector current at about 0.3 mA and the quiescent collector voltage at about 4.5 V. Ignore C2 for the moment.

The output from T1 is taken via C3 to driver T2, whose bias arrangements we will discuss later. Under quiescent conditions its base is at -2.25 V relative to the positive supply line and its emitter at -1.55 V, giving a collector current of 3.3 mA. Voltage at the top of R9 is 4.0 V, between D1 and D2 4.7 V and at the collector of T2 5.4 V. Bootstrapping R9 to the speaker rather than returning it to ground greatly increases the open-loop gain (ie, the gain without negative feedback) of the amplifier.

The output stage consists of the complementary pair T3/T4. T3 handles the positive-going excursions of input and T4 the negative-going ones. The two diodes compensate for the 0.7 V loss across the two base/emitter junctions and ensure that under quiescent conditions *both* transistors are *just* conducting.

To prevent the quiescent output voltage (at the emitters of T3/T4) from drifting too far from Vcc/2, it is used to derive the bias for T2. If the output voltage were, say, to fall, T2 would be biased (via R6/R7) further forward so

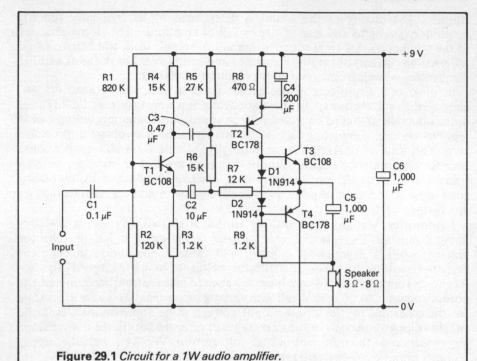

Figure 29.1 *Circuit for a 1W audio amplifier.*

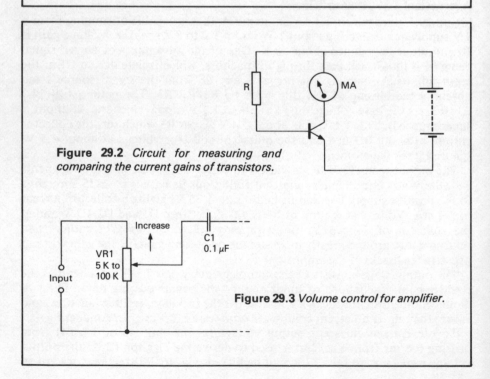

Figure 29.2 *Circuit for measuring and comparing the current gains of transistors.*

Figure 29.3 *Volume control for amplifier.*

that its collector voltage would rise (it being pnp type) restoring the required output voltage. Of course, this feedback loop would prevent the amplifier from amplifying at all if it were not *decoupled* to AF. The *decoupling* consists of capacitor C2, which could be taken straight to 'ground' from the junction of R6/R7. This filters most of the ac AF content out of the feedback loop so that nearly pure dc is fed back. Thus the output voltage is free to make the necessary *temporary* excursions associated with delivering power AF output, while any long-term tendency of the mean output voltage to deviate from that required is counteracted.

In fact C2 is taken not to ground but to the emitter of T1. The effect of this is to make R7 and R3 (via C2) an ac potential divider feeding a fraction (R7/R3) of the AF output back to the input. T1 now has the job not only of amplifying but also of comparing the scaled-down output signal applied to its emitter with the input signal being applied to its base. This kind of negative feedback is very important in AF amplifiers. Not only does it eliminate much distortion, but also it sets the voltage gain of the amplifier. Use of negative feedback makes it possible to produce large numbers of amplifiers having uniform performance, although there may be considerable differences between the individual performances of the components employed. The voltage gain of this amplifier is set at R7/R3 = 12/1.2 = 10. Since the maximum practicable excursion of the output voltage is about 4.0 V, the input signal needed to give full volume is 0.4 V.

Construction

Use Veroboard or similar. Construction is generally straightforward, but T3/T4 *must* be a matched complementary pair. Take a selection of suitable npn and pnp types and test them using the simple circuit shown in Figure 29.2. Use a 9 V battery and a selection of test resistors (R) between 10 K and 10 M. Write the collector current for each resistor against each individual transistor tested; remember to reverse the polarity of the battery and the meter for the pnp types. Hopefully you should find at least one pnp and npn transistor with similar gain characteristics. Use these as a matched complementary pair.

To test the amplifier, feed into its input some source of reasonable-quality audio material, eg, the output of a record player, radio or cassette unit. Remember that even a signal as small as 0.5 V will overload the amplifier, causing distortion, so keep the input low. If necessary, fit a volume control as shown in Figure 29.3.

Power supply

All audio equipment *must* be operated from smoothed supplies. This amplifier was designed for 9 V operation and can be run from a battery. For satisfactory operation from other voltages the values of R1, R4, R8 and R9 must be amended in accordance with the table given below.

Vcc (supply)	R1	R4	R8	R9
6 V	560 K	10 K	220 Ω	680 Ω
9 V	820 K	15 K	470 Ω	1.2 K
12 V	1.2 M	18 K	680 Ω	1.5 K
16 V	1.8 M	33 K	1 K	2.2 K
22 V	2.2 M	33 K	1.5 K	3.3 K

Parts needed (9 V version—for other supply voltages some resistor values must be changed in accordance with the table).

Semi-conductors: 2 × BC 108 or similar ⎱ including a matched
                   2 × BC 178 or similar ⎰ complementary pair (see text)
                   2 × 1N914.

Resistors: 1 × 470 Ω.
                   2 × 1.2 K.
                   1 × 12 K.
                   2 × 15 K.
                   1 × 27 K.
                   1 × 120 K.
                   1 × 820 K.

Capacitors: 1 × 0.1 μF.
                   1 × 0.47 μF.
                   1 × 10 μF 12 V.
                   1 × 200 μF 10 V.
                   2 × 1000 μF 12 V (if supply exceeds 12 V, use a 24 V type).

Project 30: Steam whistle or horn

A steam whistle generates sound by forcing high-pressure steam through a resonant pipe. Besides the musical note itself there is an accompanying hiss of escaping steam. The pitch of the note itself, however, is not constant. Its frequency is to some extent proportional to the pressure applied and, because it takes finite time to open and close the steam valve, there is a rise time (during which frequency rises) and a fall time at the end of the sounding (during which frequency falls).

The easiest way to generate a note electronically is to use a multivibrator similar to that used in Project 28 to generate the hf ac for coach lighting. The frequency, however, is rather lower: 1 kHz is suitable for a typical steam whistle—lower still for a horn. The multivibrator generates square waves which are not strictly the right *timbre* for a whistle (though not unlike a horn), but the unwanted harmonics tend to be drowned in the steam hiss, giving a final effect which is not unrealistic.

The frequency of a multivibrator is determined by a number of factors, including the supply voltage—frequency rises with voltage. Gradually (ie, over 0.3 second) building up the supply voltage on switch-on and letting it gradually decay on switch-off gives a realistic frequency shift—all that is required is to switch on the power via a suitable resistor (12 K) and shunt the supply lines via a suitable capacitor (25 μF).

The steam sound itself is generated by driving a pn junction into breakdown conditions; the most suitable junction is the base/emitter junction of a small-signal npn transistor (T1 in Figure 30.1). This produces a random electronic signal which, suitably amplified and applied to a speaker produces a loud 'steamy' hiss. T2 amplifies the hiss, a little of which is fed via R10/C6 into the multivibrator, where it partially modulates the whistle causing an attractively 'bubbly' sound. You may need to adjust the value of R10—increase it to reduce modulation—if it causes distortion of the whistle sound. Some hiss will normally pass through C4 and into the output even when the whistle is not sounding.

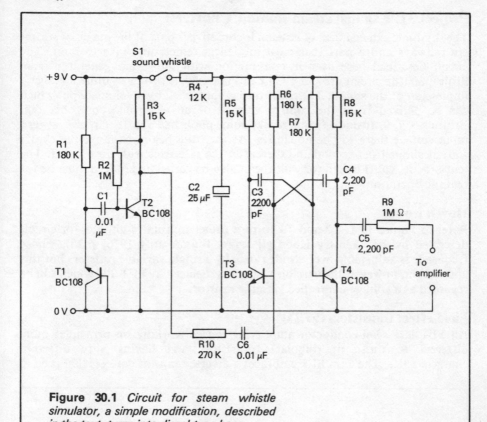

Figure 30.1 *Circuit for steam whistle simulator, a simple modification, described in the text, turns into diesel-type horn.*

Construction

Figure 29.1 gives the complete circuit. For the diesel horn omit the steam generator circuit around T1/T2 and also R4 and C2. Change the values of C3/C4 to 0.01 μF or to taste (higher for a lower note).

Veroboard construction is recommended. The circuit was developed in connection with the amplifier (Project 29) and the 'chuffer' (Project 31) and may share the same board and power supply. The recommended supply is 9 V.

Parts needed (steam whistle assumed)

Semi-conductors:	4 × BC 108 or similar.
Resistors:	1 × 12 K.
	3 × 15 K.
	3 × 180 K.
	1 × 270 K.
	2 × 1 M.
Capacitors:	3 × 2200 pF.
	2 × 0.01 μF.
Miscellaneous:	Veroboard.
	Switch.

Project 31: Exhaust steam sound ('Chuffer')

The rhythmic exhaust beat of a steam locomotive is part of the magic of steam-era railways and a part that most modellers reluctantly have to omit. The circuit described here used in conjunction with the steam generator from Project 30 (the circuit around T1/T2 in Figure 30.1) produces quite a realistic impression of the sound. The chuff rate is controlled by a voltage input which can be derived from the control voltage of an electronic controller (eg, Projects 6, 7, 9, 10 and 15) and, unlike some published chuffer circuits, at zero input voltage there will be no chuffs. As the train begins to move the chuffs start at about 1 per second and thereafter the rate rises with train speed. The 'cut-off', ie, chuff length (or width) can also be varied and indeed must be for realistic operation.

How it works

Refer to Figure 30.1. T2 and T3 form a rather unusual multivibrator circuit described by J.L. Linsley Hood (*Wireless World*, July 1976, p.36), whose frequency is adjustable over a wide range by a single variable resistor. For this application, however, the variable resistor is replaced by FET T1, which can be regarded as a voltage-controlled variable resistor.

Field-effect transistors (FETs)

An FET is a semi-conductor amplifying device working on principles quite different to those of (bipolar) transistors and having very different characteristics. The term FET embraces a diverse range of devices; that used in

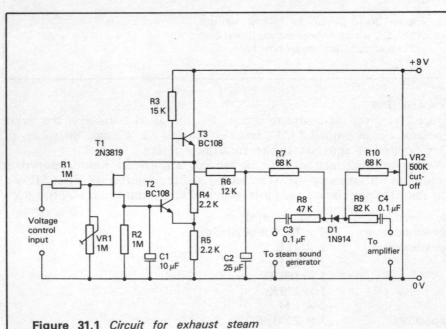

Figure 31.1 *Circuit for exhaust steam sound simulator.*

this project is a *junction-gate* FET (JUGFET or JFET) and the following remarks apply to JUGFETs but not necessarily to other FET types.

The two differences from bipolar transistors that make JUGFETs useful in this circuit are i) they are conductive when unbiased and ii) they will conduct current in either direction. Another useful difference is that input resistance is practically infinite under normal conditions, so no appreciable bias current flows.

The three terminals of a JFET corresponding to the collector, emitter and base of a bipolar transistor are called the drain, source and gate. Many JFETs including the type used in this project, are electrically symmetrical and may be operated with their drain and source terminals interchanged. Like bipolar transistors JFETs are available in two polarities: n-channel corresponding to npn and p-channel corresponding to pnp. In an n-channel device the gate must be biased negative relative to the source to reduce drain current and in a p-channel device the gate must be biased positive to reduce drain current. When sufficient gate bias is applied, drain current becomes negligible and the device is said to be 'pinched off'.

When the circuit is first switched on, C1 is uncharged so the base of T2 is at about 0 V. Consequently T2 is non-conductive and T3 is fully on, so that its emitter voltage is at about 9 V. Now T1 is a symmetrical FET so both its designated source and drain terminals may be regarded as the source. One of these is connected to the emitter of T3 and so is at about 9 V. If the gate is low, at about 0 V, the FET will be pinched off so that C1 cannot begin to charge and the circuit will remain indefinitely in this state.

As the input voltage begins to rise (as the train begins to move), the FET will begin to conduct and C1 will begin to charge via the FET. The charge rate will, of course, be determined by the gate voltage on the FET. When a certain charge voltage has been reached, T2 begins to conduct. This causes T3 to cut off, whereupon its emitter voltage falls to a low value and C1 discharges via the FET, R4 and R5. When discharge is nearly complete, the cycle repeats. Thus the circuit 'multivibrates' at a rate determined by the input voltage and the value of C1.

To convert the output of the multivibrator to 'chuffs' involves using a diode as a switch. Output of the steam hiss generator is applied via C3/R8 to the cathode of D1, while its anode is connected to a suitable amplifier via R9/C4. A diode is conductive when forward biased and non-conductive when reverse biased. The cathode of the diode is also connected via the network R6/C2/R7 to the output of the multivibrator. The anode is connected via R9 to the slider of VR2, the 'cut-off' or 'chuff width' control.

When the output of the multivibrator (ie, on the emitter of T3) is high, C2 charges up via R6—this takes about 0.3 second. During this time the cathode of D1 is taken up to about 9 V, so is reverse biased at all except the very highest settings of VR2. When the output of the multivibrator goes low, C2 discharges gradually so that the voltage on the cathode of D1 falls. When it falls below the voltage on its anode (set by VR2) it conducts and a 'chuff' begins. The 'chuff' continues until D1's cathode voltage rises again. By adjusting VR2 any chuff length from zero to continuous can be obtained. Different combinations of input voltage and VR2 setting will give effects varying from an express train at speed to a goods train struggling up a slippery gradient. For such a simple device the effect is remarkably lifelike.

Construction

Veroboard or similar is recommended. The project may share the same board and power supply as Projects 29 and 30 with which it was developed.

Operation

For testing, connect the input to the slider of a potentiometer (any value) across the supply. For normal use connect it to the control voltage of an electronic controller—adjust VR1 so that the chuffs start just as the train begins to move. Advance the cut-off control as the train accelerates or the chuffs will 'run into each other'. R9 sets the level of output (as does R9 of Project 30). You may need to adjust these values to give the correct relative loudness of whistle and exhaust steam sound.

Parts neded

Semi-conductors:	1 × 2N 3819 n-channel JFET.
	2 × BC 108 or similar.
	1 × 1N 914.
Resistors:	2 × 2.2 K.
	1 × 12 K.
	1 × 15 K.
	1 × 47 K.
	2 × 68 K.
	1 × 82 K.
	2 × 1 M.
Pots:	500 K.
	1 M pre-set.
Capacitors:	2 × 0.1 μF.
	1 × 10 μF 10 V.
	1 × 25 μF 10 V.
Miscellaneous:	Veroboard.

Part 8

Practical information and theory

Appendix 1: Tools needed for electronic projects

A number of tools are needed; as a railway modeller you may already have most of these, if not all.

A test meter

This is a meter having ac voltage, dc voltage, current and resistance ranges. The feature to look for in choosing a meter is a good selection of *current* ranges. You need ranges in multiples of 10 or less from 5 mA (or below) to 1 A (or above). Some cheaper instruments offer just two ranges: eg, 500 μA and 500 mA. This is not good enough because many of the currents used in electronics are in the range 1 to 10 mA, which would overload the lower range and barely register at all on the upper range. Do not spare the expense on your test meter; get a good one. It should give years of service and will be useful around the home and car as well.

A soldering iron

You need a conventional mains-operated iron with a miniature bit. The minimum useful element rating is 25 W; above that the higher the better. A warning lamp telling you that the iron is on is a practical safety feature.

A heavy, medium-grade file

You will need this to clean the bit of your soldering iron, which will rapidly become encrusted with oxide.

A pair of fine-nosed 'radio' pliers

These are useful for holding components while you solder them. You could use forceps, but the pliers are more comfortable and have the second valuable advantage over forceps in that, being comparatively massive, they act as a heat sink and conduct the heat away from sensitive components such as semi-conductors. If you want the heat-sinkage facility without the holding facility, put a thick rubber band around the handles of the pliers—they will 'cling' to anything.

Wire cutters

Use the proper tool for this job. I have never found the cutting edges built into pliers satisfactory. With a bit of practice you will also be able to use these for baring the ends of insulated wire, ie, stripping off the plastic or rubber sleeve at the end. Close the cutters very gently on the sleeve until you feel the greater resistance of the wire itself. Then simply pull the main length of wire away. Practise this—once you have got the knack, you'll have it for life.

In addition you will also need a craft knife, a set of miniature screwdrivers and a set of miniature drills.

Appendix 2: How to make an effective soldered joint

The most common cause of failure in amateur electronic projects is badly soldered joints. A so-called 'dry joint' looks fine and yet there is an insulating barrier of flux or grease between the items supposedly connected. The author learned the hard way; spare yourself the trouble. *There is no short cut*—you ignore the following procedure at your (or your project's) peril.

1. Clean the items to be soldered by scraping with a blade or file. This removes dirt and grease and also breaks through the thin oxide layer that forms on many metal surfaces, exposing bare metal. It is only on bare metal that solder will 'take'.
2. Tin the items to be soldered. This means applying a thin layer of solder. Touch each item in turn together with a length of solder on the hot bit of the iron. The molten solder should wet the item and when cooled give a bright, silvery appearance.
3. If possible, make a physical connection between the items being soldered, eg, twist or hook one around the other.
4. Apply the iron with more solder to the items. The solder should run smoothly into the crevices and spaces.
5. Allow the joint a minute to cool down before applying any physical stress to it, eg, using wire cutters to trim off projecting ends.
6. For electronics work use only proper electronics solder with integral flux cores.
7. When soldering a semi-conductor device, apply a heat sink (which may be the pliers in which you are holding the device) between the body of the device and the part of the lead being soldered. Complete the joint as quickly as possible—the duration of the heating is more critical than the temperature of the iron; for this reason the hotter the iron, the better, since it will enable joints to be completed more quickly.

The acrobatics of soldering

If you are unused to soldering, you may wonder just how to hold everything. Ideally you need one hand for each item being soldered, one to hold the solder and another to hold the iron; even to join two items needs four hands, which most of us do not have. The answer lies in a mixture of dexterity and ingenuity. Two items can usually be manipulated in one hand, leaving the other free for the solder. I frequently wedge the soldering iron between my knees and bring everything else to it. I have even known those who advocate holding it in their mouth—caution! Never attempt this without first ensuring that the iron is adequately earthed, otherwise a short circuit in the iron could prove lethal. (Also do not hold the solder direct in your mouth—it contains lead. If your solder comes in a plastic dispensing tube, it is, of course, safe to hold that in your mouth.)

Undoing soldered joints

The most satisfactory method in the author's experience is the use of de-soldering braid. This is a wick of copper threads impregnated with flux. Apply the iron and the end of the braid to the joint to be undone. The molten solder runs up the braid by capillary action leaving the joint free of solder and ready for separation by hand. When the end of the braid is saturated with solder, cut it off and throw it away.

Warning

So far as is practicable do your soldering well away from your model railway. If this is not possible, keep polystyrene and white-metal models under cover. A drop of molten solder falling on one of these will leave a scar that you may never eliminate. Worse still, a dropped hot soldering iron falling on a model may melt its way clean through, a thought that is almost too horrible to contemplate. So be very careful. Keep soldering irons away from young children, who find them fascinating. And be considerate of others: some people find the smell of solder irritating.

Appendix 3: Methods of construction

Nothing is more unsightly than a great tangle of components sprawling over the table top or floor. Such a construction is unsatisfactory also for more practical reasons. It is highly susceptible to breakage and to short circuits. A rigid construction method makes the circuit not only physically robust and therefore more reliable, but also more easily portable.

Many methods of construction are possible and this appendix does not claim to be comprehensive. The methods described are some that the author has tried and found satisfactory. Converting the circuit diagram into a practical reality should not prove too difficult. The physical layout need not be a copy of the layout of the circuit diagram. Provided the paths of continuity are the same, the physical layout itself is immaterial, although in practice it is generally more convenient for components electrically adjacent to be physically near.

Tagstrip

This is most appropriate for simpler circuits, eg, simple controllers and bistables. The tagstrip is a strip of paxolin bearing at intervals metal tags to which components or wires can be soldered. The leads of power transistors may need to be *gently* splayed to equal the pitch of the tags. Figure A3.1 shows the output stage of the touch-sensor controller (Project 14) using tagstrip construction; for the rest of that project, Veroboard construction is recommended.

Veroboard

Veroboard is paxolin sheet clad on the reverse with conductive copper strips at intervals (0.1 inch or 2.54 mm is the commonest pitch) with holes at the same

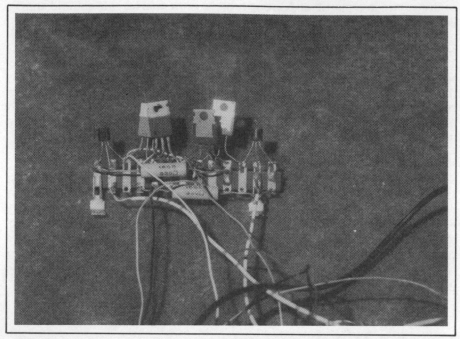

A3.1 *Output stage of the touch sensor controller (Project 14) using tagstrip construction.*

A3.2 *The rest of the touch sensor controller (Project 14) assembled on a piece of Veroboard measuring 100 × 90 mm.*

intervals. Special boards are available for certain special applications, eg, for use with integrated circuits. The components are mounted on top of the board, their leads being inserted through the holes and soldered to the copper conductor beneath.

Breaks in the copper conductors can be made using a commercial 'spot face cutter' ('stripboard cutter'), which resembles a drill bit mounted in a handle. In fact you can use a ⅛ inch drill bit, but it is more awkward. Insert the point in a hole at a suitable point on the appropriate conductor and twist the device back and forth. The result is the removal of the copper and formation of a small dent in the undersurface of the board. *Always check carefully that the break is complete*; sometimes an almost invisible whisker of copper remains closing the gap and this can wreak havoc in a circuit. Small pieces of stray copper conductor can also come to rest, short-circuiting adjacent copper conductors. Oversize blobs of solder can also cause this.

Veroboard allows components to be packed at a very high density (especially if the resistors are mounted perpendicular to the board). The whole circuit of the touch-sensor controller (Project 14) except for the output stage and the control panel can easily be accommodated on a piece of Veroboard measuring 100 × 90 mm as shown in Figure A3.2.

Blob board

This resembles Veroboard with a wider pitch (around 4 mm) and without holes. Intended for experimental rather than permanent projects, it can nevertheless be used for the latter. Components are mounted on the same side of the board as the conductors, which are pre-tinned. Conductors can be broken with a spot face cutter, but it is a time-consuming job. The system works tolerably well but guard against dry joints and blobs of solder short-circuiting adjacent conductors. Figure A3.3 shows the hf generator for coach lighting (Project 28) using Blob board construction.

Printed circuits

Commercial electronic equipment uses printed circuit boards (pcbs), but there is no reason why amateurs and even beginners should not also make them up and use them for permanent projects. It is best—at least to begin with—to buy a printed circuit board kit from an electronics supplier or from Tandy, as this will contain more detailed instructions than can be given here.

To start you need to plan—carefully!—the positions of the components on the board and the layout of the copper conductors. Double check your layout—mistakes after this stage cannot easily be rectified. Then take a piece of copper-clad board (as used for sleepers on home-made track) of the right size, clean the copper surface *thoroughly* using Vim or a similar abstergent cleaner and draw in the copper conductors using an etch-resist pen. This deposits on the board a substance rather like nail varnish. The pen will probably have a pump action to keep the etch resist flowing freely. Try to keep the thickness of the resist even.

When the etch resist has dried, float the board (copper-clad side down) in a solution of ferric chloride. Be careful with this—it is nasty stuff. The stronger and warmer the solution, the quicker the etching. The instructions in the kit will tell you how much of the crystals to dissolve in how much water, but take

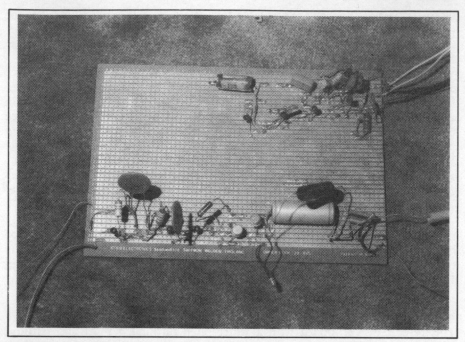

A3.3 *High-frequency generator for coach lighting (Project 28) on blob board.*

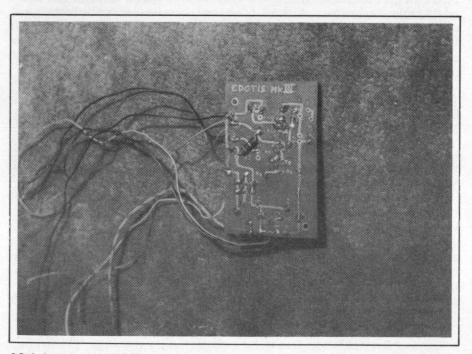

A3.4 *A prototype EDOTIS unit (Project 17) on a home made printed circuit board (reverse side).*

care as heat is generated as the solid goes into solution.

Ideally, after about five minutes, the ferric chloride will have etched the copper off the board except where it has been protected by the etch resist. Remove the board from the solution, wash it carefully in water and dry it. Remove the etch resist using nail varnish remover (acetone). Drill the holes for the component leads.

There are many variations on this process. Double-sided copper-clad board is available for especially complex circuits. Light-sensitive etch resist is available so that large numbers of identical boards can be made photographically from a master design drawn on acetate film. As on Veroboard, resistors may be mounted horizontally or vertically, depending on the space available. Printed circuit boards look good and are a robust way of assembling circuits. Figure A3.4 shows a prototype EDOTIS unit (Project 17) on a home-made pcb.

Appendix 4: The resistance/capacitance colour code and preferred values

Most resistors and also some capacitors have their value marked not in figures but in an internationally accepted colour code giving the resistance in Ohms (Ω) or capacitance in picoFarads (pF); 1,000,000 pF = 1 μF. Colour coding makes it far easier to select the right component from a box of mixed values— it saves turning each device round until the markings are located, assuming they can be located at all!

The colour code itself shows a logical sequence. Each colour represents a figure, thus:

black = 0	yellow = 4	purple = 7
brown = 1	green = 5	grey = 8
red = 2	blue = 6	white = 9
orange = 3		

Figure A4.1 shows how these colours are applied in bands on the devices. The *first* band (or its equivalent) gives the first significant figure of the value. The *second* band gives the second significant figure. The *third* band gives the exponential, ie, the number of noughts that follow the two significant figures. The following examples show how these work for *resistors*:

	orange/orange/orange	= 3 3 000	= 33 000 Ω = 33 K
	brown/black/red	= 1 0 00	= 1000 Ω = 1 K
	blue/grey/brown	= 6 8 0	= 680 Ω
	orange/white/black	= 3 9 -	= 39 Ω
BUT	yellow/purple	= 4 7	= 4.7 Ω

(NOTE! No third band)

The *fourth* band on a resistor gives its tolerance, ie, a measure of how accurately the device's actual resistance conforms to that marked on it. Brown = ± 1%; red = ± 2%; gold = ± 5%; silver = ± 10%; no fourth band = ± 20%.

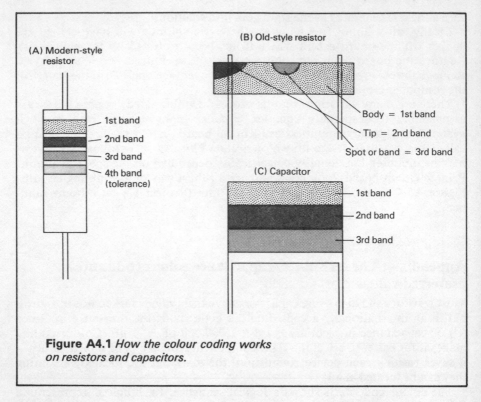

Figure A4.1 *How the colour coding works on resistors and capacitors.*

Capacitors

The colour code works in the same way giving the value in pF. Subtract 6 from the exponential to get the value in μF. Thus brown/black/yellow $= 100000 = 100\ 000$ pF $= 0.1\ \mu$F. On Mullard polyester types there is no separation between bands, so a capacitor apparently coded red/yellow but with the red band double width is in fact red/red/yellow $= 2\ 2\ 0000$ pF $= 0.22\ \mu$F.

Preferred values

Resistors and capacitors are made in standard ranges of values following a roughly logarithmic sequence. In the E12 series there are 12 values per decade; their significant figures are: 10, 12, 15, 18, 22, 27, 33, 39, 47, 56, 68, 82. In the E24 series there are 24 values per decade consisting of the E12 values given above and the following 12 intermediate values: 11, 13, 16, 20, 24, 30, 36, 43, 51, 62, 75, 91.

Resistors having all values in the E12 range from about 1.0 Ω to 10 M are quite easily obtainable; those in the other E24 values are less easy to find. Capacitors are available for all E12 values from a few pF up to about 1 μF; above this electrolytic and tantalum types are used in which working voltage also becomes important. Sometimes only alternate E12 values (ie, 10, 15, 22, 33, 47, 68) are available in any given series.

In general in electronics the values of resistors and capacitors used are not very critical. Thus, where 1 K is specified 820 Ω or 1.2 K or even 680 Ω or 1.5 K can often be used without adversely affecting the performance of the circuit.

Appendix 5: Characteristics of some popular semi-conductors

npn

Type	Case	Ptotal	Vceo	Ic	hfe	ft(MHz)	Remarks
BC 107*	TO 18	360 mW	45 V	100 mA	300	250	
BC 108*	TO 18	360 mW	20 V	100 mA	500	250	
BC 109*	TO 18	360 mW	20 V	100 mA	500	250	low noise
2N 5136*	TO 105	n/a	20 V	500 mA	100	200	
BC 182*	TO 92 (A) or (B)	300 mW	50 V	200 mA	300	150	general purpose
BC 183*	TO 92 (A) or (B)	300 mW	30 V	200 mA	500	150	
BC 184*	TO 92 (A) or (B)	300 mW	30 V	200 mA	500	150	low noise
2N 3904*	TO 92 (C)	n/a	40 V	200 mA	200	300	general purpose
ZTX 300*	E line	300 mW	25 V	500 mA	200	150	general purpose
BC 337*	TO 92 (B) or (C)	625 mW	45 V	500 mA	400	200	
BFY 50	TO 39	800 mW	35 V	1 A	30	60	general purpose
BFY 51	TO 39	800 mW	30 V	1 A	40	50	
BFY 52	TO 39	800 mW	20 V	1 A	60	50	
2N 2222*	TO 18	500 mW	30 V	600 mA	150	300	
2N 3725	TO 5	800 mW	50 V	1 A	100	450	
BD 437	TO 126	36 W	45 V	4 A	40	3	
2N 5191	TO 126	40 W	60 V	4 A	100	2	
BD 201	TO 220	60 W	45 V	8 A	30	3	
MJE 3055	TO 127	90 W	60 V	10 A	50	2.5	
2N 3055	TO 3	115 W	60 V	15 A	50	2.5	

*Can be used as substitutes for BC 108 in circuits in this book.

pnp

Type	Case	Ptotal	Vceo	Ic	hfe	ft(MHz)	Remarks
BC 177*	TO 18	300 mW	-45 V	-300 mA	150	150	complement to BC 107/8/9
BC 178*	TO 18	300 mW	-25 V	-300 mA	200	150	
BC 179*	TO 18	300 mW	-25 V	-300 mA	500	150	
2N 5142*	TO 105	n/a	-20 V	-500 mA	100	200	complement to 2N 5136
BC 212*	TO 92 (A) or (B)	300 mW	-50 V	-200 mA	150	200	complement to BC 182/3/4
BC 213*	TO 92 (A) or (B)	300 mW	-30 V	-200 mA	200	350	
BC 214*	TO 92 (A) or (B)	300 mW	-30 V	-200 mA	300	200	
2N 3906*	TO 92 (C)	n/a	-40 V	-200 mA	200	300	complement to 2N 3904
ZTX 500*	E line	300 mW	-25 V	-500 mA	200	150	complement to ZTX 300
BC 327*	TO 92 (B) or (C)	625 mW	-45 V	-500 mA	400	260	complement to BC 337
BC 461*	TO 39	1 W	-60 V	-2 A	150	50	near complement to BFY 50/1/2

*Can be used as substitutes for BC 178 in circuits in this book.

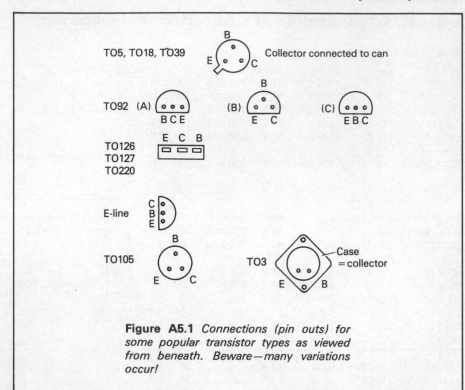

Figure A5.1 *Connections (pin outs) for some popular transistor types as viewed from beneath. Beware—many variations occur!*

Type	Case	Ptotal	Vceo	Ic	hfe	ft(MHz)	Remarks
2N 2907*	TO 18	400 mW	-30 V	-600 mA	150	300	complement to 2N 2222
2N 5022	TO 5		-80 V	-1 A	100	450	complement to 2N 3725
2N 5194	TO 126	40 W	-60 V	-4 A	100	2	complement to 2N 5191
MJE 2955	TO 127	90 W	-60 V	-10 A	50	2.5	complement to MJE 3055
MJE 2955	TO 3	115 W	-60 V	-15 A	50	2.5	complement to 2N 3055

*Can be used as substitutes for BC 178 in circuits in this book.

Key to characteristics

P*total* = total power that may be continuously dissipated by the device. The power being dissipated by a transistor equals V*ceo* × I*c* (see below).

V*ceo* = maximum voltage that may be applied continuously to the collector relative to the emitter, the base being open-circuit (unbiased).

I*c* = maximum continuous collection current.

h*fe* = typical current gain. This figure varies enormously with conditions and between individuals even of the same nominal type. Many European general-purpose transistors (ie, those having type numbers beginning BC, eg, BC 108) are sometimes graded according to gain into A (low gain), B (medium gain) and C (high gain). Thus a BC 108 C should have higher gain than a BC 108 B. A device simply marked BC 108 is ungraded and its gain may fall anywhere in the possible range.

ft = transition frequency, not a figure liable to cause concern in model railway electronics, but useful in general electronics. The current gain of transistors falls with frequency of input signal (if ac); at ft gain becomes unity, above which amplification, of course, becomes impossible.

Appendix 6: Where to get electronic components

This is an age-old problem, which gets worse as time goes by. There is no *one* answer. The following is a list of methods; no doubt you will use all of them from time to time.

Electronic components retailers

There was a time when a visit to London's Edgware Road would furnish all your needs, as there were then dozens of component shops there in close proximity. However, takeovers, mergers and moves up-market to more profitable hi-fi retailing have effectively stopped many outlets. Other shops have specialised in computer hardware and software. Edgware Road is still worth a visit if you are in London with time to spare. If you live outside London, look in *Yellow Pages* (also see below under 'Mail Order'). Many mail order suppliers also operate retail shops; there may be one near you.

Mail order

There is a multiplicity of mail order dealers throughout the UK. The best way to find their names, addresses and current prices is to consult the advertisements in popular electronics magazines that you will find in any newsagents. These include *Wireless World*, *Practical Wireless*, *Electronics Today International* and *Elektor*. If you are a real miser, and unwilling to pay for a magazine, you may be able to consult one or more of these at your local public library.

In these advertisements you will see seemingly amazing bargains. I can only advise you to watch *carefully* what is being offered. The advertisers are scrupulously fair in their wording: a bag of '100 unmarked, untested transistors' will contain just that. Even if you establish which are working npn types, working pnp types and non-functional devices—which you can do with tedious testing—you will still not know the current ratings and voltage ratings of the working devices. My experience has been that devices from this kind of special offer are not reliable—many are manufacturers' rejects—and will give trouble if used in the kind of projects described in this book. Model railway circuits demand full-specification devices and readers are urged—for their own satisfaction and sanity!—to use only marked, tested devices. Even among these, there are still bargains to be had. (The author recently bought 200 marked, tested transistors at $2\frac{1}{2}$p each and these have proved quite satisfactory). By all means go for the bargains—but make sure that they *are* bargains—*know* what you are getting.

Compare mail order suppliers' prices with caution. Most charge extra for postage and packing. Some have a minimum order charge. Some include VAT in their advertised prices; with others you must add it. So when you see supplier A advertising an item at 10p and supplier B advertising the same at 12p, supplier B may nevertheless be cheaper.

Tandy (known as Radio Shack in the USA)

This is the closest that there is to an electronics chain store—the Tandy store is a familiar sight in High Streets throughout the UK and overseas. The range of electronic components stocked is limited and the regular prices tend to be high. Nevertheless if there is one item that you need, it is clearly cheaper and more convenient to pay 80p across the counter at your local Tandy than 35p from a mail order supplier who adds a 50p charge for postage and packing. Tandy operates more gimmicks than the rest of the shops on an average High Street put together; these include a multiplicity of sales throughout the year advertised by leaflets sent through the post (they take your name and address whenever you make a purchase) and a free battery club. In the sales there are genuine bargains to be had; also *some* items in the regular catalogue undoubtedly offer exceptional value for money. My experience with my local store (which I plague with requests for obscure items) has been that time and time again the staff have gone out of their way to be helpful.

Local radio shops

Radio shops which operate a repair service of necessity carry stocks of components, but they do not exist to serve the needs of electronics buffs! In dire emergency, when your project needs a certain component to finish it off, try your local radio shop, but his prices are likely to be high.

Ex-equipment components

Much old electronic equipment, especially old TV sets, is ditched—sometimes, regrettably, literally in the local ditch! Nowadays a discarded TV set is quite likely to be transistorised and to have up-to-date components. The local civic amenities tip is another source of these. Market stalls and junk shops sometimes sell ex-equipment circuit boards, often from computers. Remove the useful looking components following the procedure given near the end of Appendix 2. A warning—it gets a bit tedious after a while. On a purely economic basis you would probably be better off spending an equivalent time in paid employment and using your pay to buy new components. This is, of course, why these panels are often simply thrown away.

While there is no problem with the resistors and capacitors that you amass in this way, the semi-conductors may have unfamiliar type numbers. You will need access to a semi-conductor data book—there may be one in your local public library's reference section. Some radio and TV transistors will be unsuitable for most model railway applications, especially those having type numbers beginning AF or BF, eg, AF117, BF194. Keep these—one day you might want to build a radio.

Friends

Unless you live on a lighthouse or in the middle of a desert, you probably have a large circle of friends and colleagues (at work, school, church, club, pub, next door, etc) which is nowadays *bound* to include at least one other electronics buff who has a stock of components. I suggest that you make yourself known to him and swop notes on what you are doing. While I *do not* recommend scrounging, there is nevertheless a fraternal bond that links electronics buffs, just as there is between railway modellers. One of the unwritten rules of this informal bond is that if you are desperate for a certain component and your friend has a spare one, he gives it to you. (That is unless it is a highly expensive item and so far as the projects in this book are concerned, none comes in that category.) This bond entails reciprocality: when next week your friend is desperate for something that you have, you are obliged to give it to him, and so on. This kind of informal co-operation can help enormously, especially while you are wondering if that massive mail order consignment has gone astray in the post!

Appendix 7: Electronics theory I: Current, voltage, resistance and power

Electric current

An electric current consists of a stream of electrons flowing along a suitable conductor. It is conventional to regard the current as flowing out of the positive terminal of the power supply, through the circuit (the *load*) and returning into the negative terminal of the power supply. In fact each electron bears a negative charge and the direction of flow of the electrons themselves is contrary to that of 'conventional current', ie, from the negative terminal of the power supply through the circuit to the positive terminal.

The unit of electric current is the *Ampère*, commonly abbreviated Amp or just A. Smaller units of current commonly used in electronics are the milliampere (mA) which equals $1/1,000$ A and the microAmpere (μA) which equals $1/1,000,000$ A or $1/1,000$ mA. This *amperage* is an expression of the *rate of flow* of electricity—indeed 1 A corresponds to 6.24×10^{18} electrons per second passing the measuring point.

There are some simple rules relating to the behaviour of electric current. Current can neither be created nor destroyed at any point in the circuit. The current flowing into any component must equal that flowing out. More rules follow when we consider electromotive force and resistance.

Electromotive force (EMF)

Just as tractive force must be applied to railway vehicles to make them roll, so a force must be applied to the electrons in a conductor to set them moving. A force that sets electrons in motion is called simply an *electromotive force* (EMF) and its unit is the Volt (after Voltère), usually abbreviated V. Small units of voltage are the milliVolt (mV) equalling $1/1,000$ V and the microvolt equalling $1/1,000,000$ V or $1/1,000$ mV.

Common sources of EMF in a circuit are a battery or a dynamo or the secondary winding of a transformer. Notice that *inside the source of EMF* the electrons arriving at the positive terminal (or the terminal that for the time being is positive in an ac circuit) are propelled to the negative terminal contrary to the normal direction of electron flow in the load circuit.

Resistance

When a source of EMF, eg, a battery, is connected to a circuit, the magnitude of the current that flows depends not only on the voltage of the EMF but also on the nature of the circuit. For many circuits, current is proportional to voltage, so that the ratio of voltage to current is constant for that circuit; such circuits are said to be *linear*. This voltage-divided-by-current figure is known as the *resistance* of the circuit and is measured in Ohms, abreviated Ω. Larger units of resistance are the kilOhm (K) which equals 1,000 Ω and the megOhm (M) which equals 1,000,000 Ω or 1,000 K.

Ohm's law

Ohm's law states that for linear circuits current is proportional to voltage and inversely proportional to resistance. This may be expressed algebraicly:

$$I = \frac{E}{R} \text{ or } R = \frac{E}{I} \text{ or } E = IR$$

where *I* equals current, *E* equals EMF and *R* equals resistance.

Conveniently the equation holds good when *I* is in Amps, *E* in Volts and *R* in Ohms. So we could rewrite the equation as follows:

$$A = \frac{V}{\Omega} \text{ or } \Omega = \frac{V}{A} \text{ or } V = A \Omega$$

Usefully in electronics it still holds good when *I* is in mA and *R* in K (and when *I* is in μA and R in M). So:

$$mA = \frac{V}{A} \text{ or } K = \frac{V}{mA} \text{ or } V = mAK$$

Ohm's law is of such fundamental importance in electronics that the above equations should be committed to memory. They appear over and over again.

Resistances in series

Figure A7.1 shows two resistors in series. The current flows through first 1 K then 2 K. It is not hard to see that this is equivalent to flowing through one 3 K resistor. (So, in this circuit, current by Ohm's law is 12 V/3 K = 4 mA.) For any number of resistances in series the general formula is:

$$R_{total} = R_1 + R_2 + R_3 + R_4 + R_5 + \ldots$$

Resistances in parallel

Figure A7.2 shows two resistors in parallel connected to the same power supply. We can therefore calculate the current flowing through each individually by Ohm's law.

$$\text{For } R_1 \; I_1 = 12 \, V/1 \, K = 12 \, mA$$
$$\text{For } R_2 \; I_2 = 12 \, V/2 \, K = 6 \, mA$$

The total current drained from the battery is 12 + 6 = 18 mA. So the two parallel resistors behave as one resistor having a resistance of 12 V/18 mA = 0.67 K = 670 Ω. Had the two resistors had the same value, the combined current would have been double the individual ones, making the combined resistance exactly half the individual values. Indeed for *n* parallel resistances each of value *R* the total resistance is *R/n*

In fact when resistances are in parallel, their individual currents, each

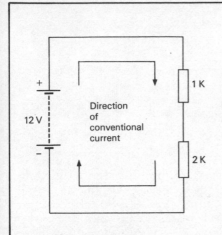

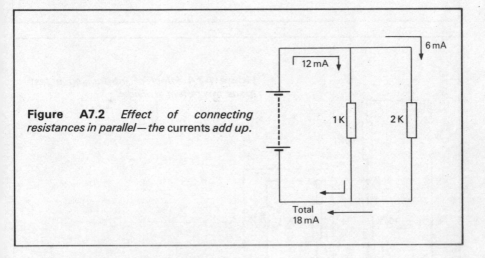

Figure A7.1 *Resistances in series add up—the current flow through a total of 1K + 2K = 3K.*

Figure A7.2 *Effect of connecting resistances in parallel—the* currents *add up.*

inversely proportional to resistance, add up to give a combined current inversely proportional to total resistance. This is summarised in the general formula for parallel resistances:

$$\frac{1}{R_{\text{total}}} = \frac{1}{R_1} + \frac{1}{R_2} + \frac{1}{R_3} + \frac{1}{R_4} + \frac{1}{R_5} + \cdots$$

There is a more convenient form for two resistances in parallel:

$$R_{\text{total}} = \frac{R_1 \times R_2}{R_1 + R_2}$$

By applying the appropriate equations the total resistance of any series/parallel resistance network can be calculated. This is of direct practical value to the experimenter, since it may enable him to make up a required resistance from series/parallel combinations when a suitable single component is unavailable.

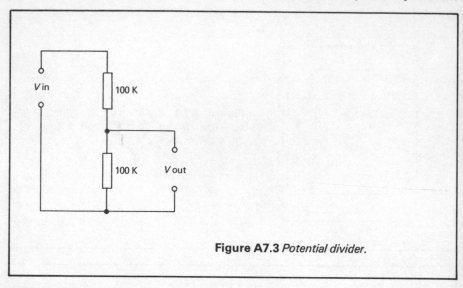

Figure A7.3 *Potential divider.*

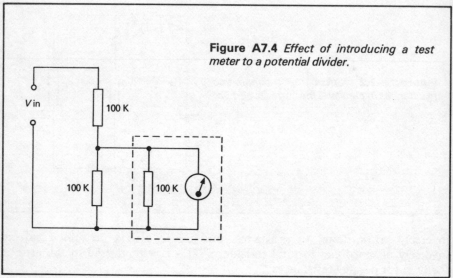

Figure A7.4 *Effect of introducing a test meter to a potential divider.*

Potential difference (PD)

When a current flows through a resistance, a voltage is set up across the resistance, which may be calculated by Ohm's law: $IR = E$. This voltage is known as a *potential difference* (PD). The distinction between PD and EMF is not always easy to understand, especially as both are measured as voltages. There are, however, several differences. An EMF is the force that drives a current and its voltage remains even if the current is switched off; a PD in contrast is the consequence of a current and disappears if the current is switched off. Inside the source of an EMF, electrons move from the positive to the negative terminal; inside the resistance across which a PD is developed the electrons flow from negative to positive.

Potential dividers

Consider the circuit shown in Figure A7.3. Suppose V_{in} (the input voltage) is 12 V and both resistors are 100 K. The combined resistance of the two resistors is $100 + 100 = 200$ K so the current flowing is 12 V/200 K = 60 μA. The PD raised across each resistor is 100 K $\times$ 60 μA = 6 V. In fact two series resistors form a *potential divider* in which any output voltage (V_{out}) between zero and V_{in} can be obtained by choice of values for R_1 and R_2.

$$V_{out} = \frac{R_2}{R_1 + R_2} \times V_{in}$$

There is, however, a hidden danger in potential dividers. Allowance must be made for the resistance of the circuit connected to V_{out}. For instance, in the example given above suppose that a voltmeter having input resistance of 100 K (a typical value) were connected to V_{out} to check the output of the potential divider. Its 100 K would now be in parallel with R_2 and would upset the operation of the potential divider as Figure A7.4 shows. The parallel combination R_2/R_V would behave as a 50 K resistor and V_{out} would become:

$$\frac{50}{100 + 50} \times 12 = 4\,\text{V}$$

If the test were repeated taking the output from R1, the same result would be obtained. So we should have the ludicrous but all-too-real situation: voltage across R1 = indicated 4 V, across R2 = indicated 4 V, across R1 + R2 = indicated 12 V; therefore $4 + 4 = 12$! When using a test meter always allow for the possibility that the instrument itself may introduce inaccuracies into the circuit. With voltmeters a high input resistance is an advantage in this respect. When using potential dividers, ensure that the output resistor is low compared to the input resistance of the circuit to which it is to be connected.

Power

The amount of *power* in a circuit is proportional to both the voltage applied and the current flowing:

$$P = EI$$

where P is power. The unit of power is the *Watt* (after steam pioneer James Watt) abbreviated W; the milliwatt (mW) is also used—1 mW = 1/1,000 W. Conveniently W = V A. So a model locomotive drawing 250 mA from a controller delivering 8 V (typical figures) is consuming 8 V $\times \frac{1}{4}$ A = 2 W.

Power calculations are important in determining choice of components. Many smaller resistors are rated for $\frac{1}{4}$ W (= 250 mW). Consider a 330 Ω resistor in a circuit where 6 V is applied across it. By Ohm's law the current is 6 V/0.33 K = 18 mA approximately. Power dissipation therefore is 6 V $\times$ 18 mA = 108 mW, well within the rating of a $\frac{1}{4}$ W device. But if the voltage were raised to 9 V, the current would also rise to 27 mA and the dissipation would now be 9 V $\times$ 27 mA = 243 mW, almost at the limits of the device's rating; any further increase would risk overloading the device. Many smaller transistors are rated for 200 mW or 300 mW dissipation and care must be taken to prevent overloading which could cause costly failures.

Appendix 8: Electronics theory II: ac, capacitance and inductance

Alternating current (ac)

The EMFs considered in Appendix 7 were assumed to be sources of steady voltage, which drive steady currents through circuits having constant resistance; the direction of the current, of course, is determined by the polarity of the EMF. This kind of one-way current is called *direct current* (dc). It is the kind of current that a battery delivers.

The mains in the UK, most parts of Europe and the USA supplies *alternating current* (ac). This is current that keeps changing its direction. If we take a typical mains supply (240 V ac, 50 Hz), call one side of the supply zero and monitor the voltage on the other side relative to the first, we should obtain a pattern like that shown in Figure A8.1. The figure shows two complete *cycles*, each consisting of a positive-going peak and a negative-going trough. There are on average 50 such cycles per second; this figure is called the *frequency* and is measured in Herz (Hz), the number of Hz being the number of cycles per second. Notice that the very tips of the peaks and the very bottoms of the troughs exceed the nominal mains voltage; they reach about 340 V for a 240 V nominal supply. This is because the nominal mains voltage is an *average* figure, known as the root mean square (rms). Since there are two instants in each mains cycle when the voltage delivered is zero, there must also be times when the voltage delivered exceeds 240 V if that average value is to be maintained. The rms figure could be defined as the value of the dc supply which would deliver an equal amount of power into a circuit of given resistance over an appreciable period of time. It is also the figure indicated by a test meter connected to an ac supply. This difference between the peak figure and the rms figure is important in the design of power supplies (see Appendix 9).

Capacitance

Capacitors and their ability to store electricity (their *capacitance*) were briefly introduced in Project 3. Some further information on their performance is given here. The unit of capacitance is the Farad (F), named after physicist Michael Faraday, but the Farad itself is a massive unit rarely encountered. Most capacitors used in general electronics have values in microFarads (μF) and in radio some have values in picoFarads (pF). 1,000,000 pF = 1 μF; 1,000,000 μF = 1 F.

When a capacitor is connected via a resistor to a dc EMF, it takes appreciable time to charge up. It would be most useful to know how long it takes to become fully charged. The question, however, is meaningless, because it *never* gets *fully* charged. As charge-up proceeds, the charge current diminishes, slowing down the charging process. As full charge is approached, the rate of charge becomes negligible. So in theory *infinite* time would be needed to charge the capacitor fully. Exactly the same is true of its discharge.

Instead electronic engineers work on the basis of a 63% charge or discharge. The time taken for a capacitor to charge up to 63% of the charging EMF or to discharge (assuming that it was practically fully charged) by 63%, ie, to 37% of the original charging voltage gives a useful working parameter; moreover, the mathematics is simple.

The time taken to charge a capacitor of C Farads to 63% (or to discharge it

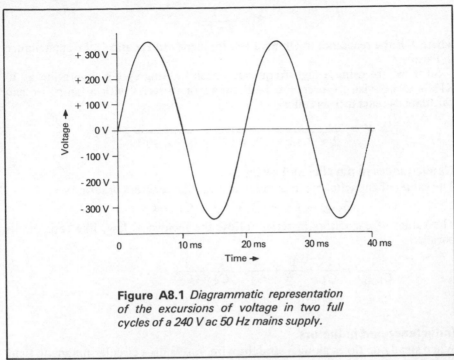

Figure A8.1 *Diagrammatic representation of the excursions of voltage in two full cycles of a 240 V ac 50 Hz mains supply.*

to 37%) of the charging EMF via a resistance of R Ohms is RC seconds. This figure is called the *time constant* for that resistor/capacitor combination and is independent of the EMF value. (Raising the EMF raises the charging current proportionately, but also raises the target voltage proportionately.) So in a voltage control system (Project 13), if the control voltage capacitor is 220 μF and the inertia control is set so that it introduces 50 K into its charge-up path, the time taken for the train to reach full speed from rest will be

$$220 \times 10^{-6} \times 50 \times 10^{3} = 11 \text{ seconds.}$$

As a capacitor charges, its effective resistance rises. As it approaches full charge-up, its effective resistance becomes practically infinite. So any attempt to pass steady dc through a capacitor will be foredoomed to failure. However, capacitors *do* conduct ac. This is because each complete cycle of ac causes a charge-up, a discharge, a recharge with opposite polarity and a further discharge. In an ac circuit a capacitor behaves to some extent like a resistor. Its ac resistance is called its *reactance* and is measured in Ohms.

Increasing the capacitance means that a greater current will be consumed in charge-up, hence a *lower* reactance. So reactance is inversely proportional to capacitance, but reactance also depends on the frequency of the ac. There will inevitably be some resistance in the circuit so that it will have a time constant as described above. A low-frequency half cycle, occupying a period longer than the circuit's time constant will more completely charge the capacitor, raising its resistance, than a high-frequency half cycle which has ended with the capacitor only partially charged and still conductive. So reactance is inversely proportional to frequency. A constant, 2π, completes the formula for reactance (X).

$$X = \frac{1}{2\pi f C}$$

where X is the reactance in Ohms, f the frequency in Hz and C the capacitance in Farads.

So if we are using a high-frequency coach lighting system operating at 30 KHz and we wish to insert a $0.1\text{-}\mu F$ capacitor in series with a lamp, we can calculate its reactance as follows:

$$X = \frac{1}{2 \times 3.14 \times 30 \times 10^3 \times 0.1 \times 10^{-6}} = 53\ \Omega.$$

Capacitances in parallel and series
The values of capacitances in parallel add up, like resistors *in series*:

$$C_{total} = C_1 + C_2 + C_3 + C_4 + C_5 + \ldots$$

The values of capacitors in series follow the reciprocal law, like resistors in parallel:

$$\frac{1}{C_{total}} = \frac{1}{C_1} + \frac{1}{C_2} + \frac{1}{C_3} + \frac{1}{C_4} + \frac{1}{C_5} + \ldots$$

Inductance and inductors
When steady dc flows along a straight wire, it sets up a circular magnetic field in a plane at right angles to the wire. Normally this field is too weak to have any practical importance. However, if the wire is wound into a coil, the magnetic field is concentrated inside the core of the coil, greatly magnifying its effect. If a rod of soft iron or ferrite is inserted into the core, this further concentrates the magnetic field, turning the coil into an *electromagnet.*

A steady magnetic field has no effect on a stationary wire passing through it, but if the wire moves relative to the field or if the field varies in its strength, an EMF will be induced in it. Note that this *change* or *movement* of the field relative to the wire is essential to the induction of an EMF. If the wire is formed into a coil and the magnet moves along the axis of the coil or parallel to it, the induced EMF will be greatly magnified, since each turn of the coil acts as a separate 'generator' and all act in series. The ability of a magnetic field to set up an EMF in a conductor is called *inductance.*

Even in the absence of an external magnet a coil exhibits electrical properties different from those of the same length of wire if it were not coiled. This is because the magnetic field set up by a varying electric current within each turn of the coil varies in proportion with the current and, being a varying magnetic field, it acts upon adjacent turns of the coil and induces in them an EMF *of opposite polarity to the EMF driving the original current.* Of course, this is of no consequence when steady dc is flowing through the coil, since the magnetic field will be steady and therefore without effect. But when an EMF is first applied to the coil and when it is disconnected, there is an effect.

Let us assume that the dc resistance of the coil is low, as is likely. When an EMF is first applied, the current flowing in the coil will attempt to rise very rapidly from zero to that which one would expect from the strict application of Ohm's law. This rapidly rising current sets up around each turn of the coil a magnetic field of rapidly rising intensity. This magnetic field of rapidly rising intensity acts on adjacent turns of the coil to induce in them a rapidly rising EMF which opposes the external EMF and reduces the current. However it does not succeed in completely stopping the current; if it did, the current could not begin to flow in the first place. Once the current has begun to flow the *rate of change* of flow declines and the induced contrary EMF fades away. So the effect of the inductance of the coil is to make the current build-up gradual.

When the external EMF is disconnected, the current passing through the coil is reduced to zero instantaneously, causing an instantaneous collapse of the magnetic field. This induces in the coil a considerable EMF *of the same polarity* (relative to the coil) as the original external source of EMF; this is known as the *inductive overshoot* or *inductive kickback*. This phenomenon can cause problems with certain designs of pulsed controller; this is considered in Part 2.

Inductance is measured in Henrys (H) but inductors (coils) as discrete components are rarely met in model railway electronics. As coils form part of transformers, relays and electric motors, however, some knowledge of their properties is useful. When an ac EMF is applied to an inductor, the same 'delay' is experienced as with dc, but now that 'delay' assumes far greater importance, since the current may hardly have begun to flow before the half cycle finishes and an opposite-polarity half cycle begins, whereupon the 'delay' begins all over again. Consequently an inductor which appears to have a low resistance to dc may nevertheless present a very high resistance to ac. This form of ac resistance like that of capacitors is known as *reactance*; it is proportional both to inductance and to frequency.

$$X = 2 \pi f L$$

where X is reactance in Ohms, f is frequency in Hz and L is inductance in Henrys.

Transformers

If two separate coils are wound on the same core so that there is efficient magnetic coupling between them, the application of an ac EMF to one winding (called the *primary*) will result in an ac EMF being induced in the other winding (called the *secondary*). Moreover, the voltages in the two windings will be in proportion to the numbers of turns. Thus, if a primary having 240 turns is connected to a mains supply of 240 V ac, a secondary having 16 turns, will deliver 16 V ac. Such a combination of two coils is called a *transformer*.

If the secondary of a transformer is left *open circuit*, ie, not forming part of a complete circuit so that no current can flow, very little current will flow in the primary; the primary will in fact exhibit the high reactance that one would expect in a massive inductor. If the secondary is connected to a suitable load so that the magnetic field set up by the primary can be used to induce current in the secondary, the reactance of the primary will be lower and more current will flow in it. Most commercial transformers are efficient exchangers of power; little power is wasted in them, so the current flowing in the primary and secondary will be inversely proportional to the voltages across them. To return to the example quoted earlier; if the primary voltage is 240 V and the secondary 16 V and if the secondary is delivering 240 mA, then the current in the primary should be 16 mA.

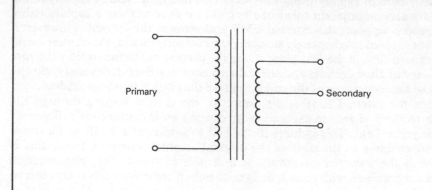

Figure A8.2 *Symbol for a typical transformer. This symbol suggests a step-down transformer with a centre-tapped secondary.*

Transformers are used extensively for stepping high mains voltages down to lower voltages for such applications as power supplies for model railways and electronic equipment. Figure A8.2 shows the circuit diagram symbol for a typical transformer; it is quite usual for transformers to have tappings on both primary and secondary windings (or to have more than one secondary winding) so that they can be used with a variety of primary voltages (generally mains supplies) to obtain a variety of output voltages. In the diagrammatic symbol it is usual to draw one winding with a greater number of turns than the other (assuming it is a step-down or step-up transformer) but in the diagram the ratio need not be the same as that of the device represented.

Electromagnets, solenoids and relays

As we have seen, an electric current flowing in a coil produces a powerful magnetic field in the core. One useful application for this is as an *electromagnet*, ie, a magnet whose magnetism can be switched on and off. Polarity of the magnetic field will depend on the polarity of the supply, but if it is simply the device's ability to attract ferrous metal objects that is wanted, polarity is immaterial and the electromagnet will work satisfactorily on ac or dc power supplies. Electromagnets suspended from cranes are used by scrap metal dealers for separating ferrous and non-ferrous metals. In a model railway a working electromagnet can be used to great effect to add interest to a lineside scrapyard.

It is as a *solenoid* that an electromagnet is most likely to be encountered by the railway modeller (setting aside for the moment its crucial rôle in the heart of every dc motor). A solenoid consists of an electromagnet with a captive iron bolt in its core. The bolt is free to slide in and out of the core. When current is applied to an electromagnet, the bolt is drawn further into the core. When the current is stopped, the bolt may return to its former position by spring action or gravity or it may remain in its new position until a second electromagnet is energised which draws it back. Solenoids are widely used in model railways as turnout (point) motors and for operating semaphore signals and other accessories. Electronic circuitry for their operation is described in Project 22.

One particular application of a solenoid is a *relay*. In a relay the moving bolt (the *armature*) is used to operate a bank of switches (usually electrically insulated from the coil). Relays were at one time widely used in telephone exchanges and for other applications that involved complex multiple switching. They are still common in model railway electrical systems, but for many of these applications they may be replaced by electronic switching which offers lower cost, lower power consumption and greater reliability.

Electric motors

Electric motors are, of course, of fundamental importance to model railways and therefore, although not strictly a part of electronics, their operation needs some consideration. There are many types of electric motor, but only dc types as used in model locomotives will concern us here.

A dc motor has essentially two parts: a fixed *stator* consisting of one or two permanent magnets and a rotating *armature* positioned within the magnetic field. Mounted on the armature are three or five (or occasionally seven) coils called, confusingly, the *poles*. Also mounted on the armature are the segments (as many as the poles) of the *commutator* to which the ends of the pole windings are connected. The segments contact the *brushes*, two in number, mounted on the stator and connected to the terminals of the motor.

When an EMF is applied to the terminals of the motor all but one of the pole windings is energised. The energised poles act as electromagnets, being attracted to one (side of the) permanent magnet and repelled from the other. Consequently they begin to move, causing the armature to rotate. As an energised winding approaches a magnet to which it is attracted, the switching action of the commutator removes its power supply so that the attraction disappears. (If this did not happen, the energised pole would stop adjacent to the magnet, preventing further the rotation). As its supply disappears, another pole winding is energised and the process is repeated. So rotation continues as long as sufficient power is supplied, all the poles becoming energised in turn by the commutator. Reversing the polarity of the power supply reverses the polarity of the pole windings, but not that of the permanent magnet(s), so that all the former attractions become repulsions and *vice versa* and the direction of rotation is reversed. Reference to Figure A8.3 may clarify the sequence of operation.

An electric motor will, of course, demonstrate all the electrical properties to be expected of a predominantly inductive device. For instance it will exhibit inductive overshoot and in certain circuits precautions must be taken to prevent this from interfering with the operation of the controller. Since a motor includes coils rotating in a magnetic field, it also behaves as a generator, even when it is being used as a motor. Its rotation causes it to generate an EMF which opposes that of the power supply and tends to reduce the current consumed; this is called the *back EMF* and, other factors being equal, the back EMF is proportional to motor speed. This is useful, since it is possible to design an electronic controller which monitors the back EMF and compares it with a control voltage in order to achieve highly accurate speed control.

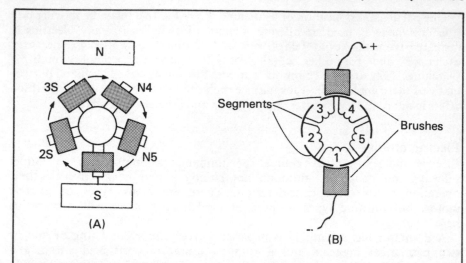

Figure A8.3 *Five-pole, single-magnet dc motor: (a) cross section through poles and (b) cross section through commutator at the same moment. Pole 1 is not energised; arrows indicate magnetic forces, hence direction of rotation. Poles 2 and 3 are connected in series at the moment, as are poles 4 and 5.*

Appendix 9: Semi-conductor diodes

Strictly speaking the term *semi-conductor* refers to a group of substances including silicon, germanium and alloys of gallium with phosphorus or arsenic or both, which are intermediate in conductivity between those substances normally considered conductors and those regarded as insulators. From the substance, however, the term has come to be applied to a diversity of electronic components which utilise the peculiar properties of semi-conducting materials; those that we shall be considering are junction diodes, bipolar transistors and field-effect transistors (FETS).

Semi-conductor action

The mode of action of semi-conductor devices is exceedingly complex and the reader wishing to have a detailed explanation should consult more comprehensive works on the subject. An exact understanding, however, is not needed in order to apply the devices correctly in electronic circuitry, so only a brief explanation will be given here. Silicon is the semi-conducting material in most general use, but references here to silicon can generally be taken to apply to other semi-conductor materials and devices, unless differences are specified.

Chemically pure silicon is a poor conductor of electricity because its atoms interlock in its crystal structure in such a way that there are no free electrons available to act as 'carriers' of electric current; in this respect it resembles those materials generally termed insulators. It is possible, however, to introduce trace impurities into silicon which affect its electrical properties. The atoms of these impurities replace silicon atoms in the crystal structure, but they have different numbers of electrons. Certain impurities, such as arsenic, have surplus electrons thereby introducing 'free' electrons into the silicon, giving it a negative charge; such silicon is called *n-type*. Other impurities, such as boron, have a deficit of electrons and introduce what are called *holes* into the silicon. These holes are the positively charged gaps into which electrons fit and which attract electrons; such silicon has an overall positive charge and is called *p-type*. When an electron enters a hole, their opposite charges cancel each other. When an atom with a hole succeeds in attracting an electron from a neighbouring atom, a new hole is created in the atom which it left. Thus holes appear to wander through a p-type silicon, just as electrons do through n-type silicon. Since the flow of holes is a consequence of the movement of electrons, this too constitutes an electric current, but since holes bear effective positive charges, the flow of holes is in the same direction as conventional current flow.

Both n-type and p-type silicon are, of course, conductive, because of the presence in them of carrier electrons or holes. Individually their electrical properties are unremarkable, but if, say, an n-type impurity is introduced into one end of a piece of p-type silicon, an interface between n-type and p-type regions is formed. Such an interface is called a *pn junction* and its electrical properties are remarkable.

Some electrons, naturally enough, migrate from the negatively charged n-region across the junction to the p-region and some holes similarly from the p-region to the n-region. Thus the n-region, having lost electrons and gained holes, becomes positively charged relative to the p-region—it acts as if a battery were connected across it with its positive terminal to the n-type region. This charge cannot be measured directly on a voltmeter, but its effect is felt when the junction is being used in a circuit. This charge is responsible for the *offset voltage*, for which allowance must be made when designing circuits and choosing component values. For a silicon junction the offset voltage is around 0.7 V, for a germanium junction around 0.2 V and for a gallium-arsenic-phosphide junction around 1.8 V.

This PD across the junction establishes an effective barrier across it—the negative charge on the p-type material deters further electrons from crossing from the n-region, while the positive charge on the n-region deters further holes from making the crossing. Indeed such is the charge that electrons in the n-region tend to stay away from the junction, as do holes in the p-region. So a zone is established around the junction which is largely free of carriers (electrons and holes). Such a zone is called a *depletion area* and, since it lacks carriers, it is, like pure silicon, a very poor conductor of electricity.

This, then, is the state existing in a silicon junction *in vacuo*. Let us now see what happens when an external EMF is connected to it. If a pn junction is connected to a battery with its positive terminal to the n-region and its negative terminal to the p-region, the external battery's EMF will reinforce the internal charge which established the depletion zone around the junction, making it even wider and the junction will be even less conductive. The junction is now said to be *reverse-biased*; the only current that flows is a leakage current which for practical purposes is negligible.

If the reverse bias across the junction is increased, at a certain critical reverse voltage depending on the design of the junction the potential barrier will break down and current will flow. This is called the *breakdown* point and the reader

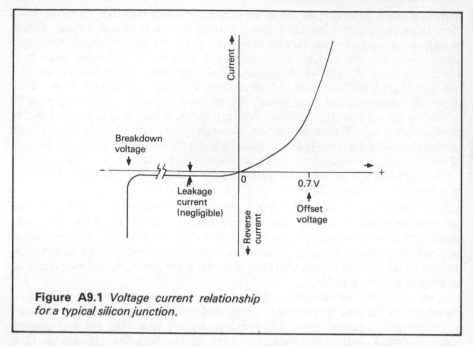

Figure A9.1 *Voltage current relationship for a typical silicon junction.*

may be excused for supposing that operating a junction beyond its breakdown point causes irreparable damage to it. Provided that precautions are taken to limit the breakdown current (and hence the power dissipated as heat in the junction), there is no damage. When the reverse bias is removed, the potential barrier is restored and the junction will function normally again. Junctions can be designed to have any breakdown voltage from zero to minus several hundreds of volts. Use is made of this property in voltage-reference ('Zener') diodes.

If we now reverse the connections to the external battery, so that its positive terminal is connected to the p-region and its negative terminal to the n-region, the junction is said to be *forward-biased*. The external EMF now reduces that of the internal fictitious battery and therefore the depletion zone becomes smaller. If the external EMF exceeds the offset voltage, the depletion zone with its potential barrier disappears altogether, so that electrons can cross freely from the n-region to the p-region and holes can cross in the opposite direction. Electrons leaving the n-region and crossing to the p-region are replaced by electrons flowing from the negative terminal of the battery, while those arriving in the n-region flow on towards the positive terminal of the battery. So a substantial electric current flows.

To summarise, then, a pn junction when reverse biased is hardly conductive (provided its breakdown voltage is not exceeded)—it presents a very high resistance. When forward biased it becomes conductive and, when its offset voltage is exceeded, it presents a very low resistance. Figure A9.1 shows in graphic form the current-voltage relationship of a typical pn junction. Since the current flowing is not proportional to the voltage applied, a pn junction does not obey Ohm's law; its resistance varies according to the EMF applied so is non-linear.

The junction diode

The simplest semi-conductor device is called a *junction diode*; it consists simply of a pn junction in a glass or epoxy resin or metal capsule. Diodes are used for a diversity of applications including power rectifiers, voltage regulators, indicator lamps and even as variable capacitors. Their most common application, however, is in switching.

Most small-signal diodes are encapsulated in glass envelopes, the cathode end (the n-type region) being marked by a coloured band or spot on the body of the device. Bags of unmarked, untested diodes can often be purchased more cheaply than branded, tested diodes; in general most of the devices in the bag will prove to be serviceable. They should be tested using a resistance meter. In the reverse direction the reading should be infinite, ie, no deflection whatsoever. Do not handle both leads of the device simultaneously while testing or you may get a spurious reading. Discard any devices that show a leakage current—you will probably find suitable non-electrical uses for them on your model railway. In the forward direction, if your resistance meter uses a 1.5 V battery, you should get a resistance reading of about half-full-scale deflection for a silicon diode and nearly full-scale-deflection for a germanium diode. As diodes are non-linear the actual resistance reading obtained will vary widely according to the characteristics of the test meter. When the diode is forward biased, the red or positive lead of the test meter is connected to the *cathode* lead of the device; this should now be marked with a blob or band of paint. Doing this now will save a lot of frustrating polarity checking later when you suddenly need a number of diodes in a complex project.

Rectifiers and power supplies

One of the most frequent switching applications for diodes is rectifying, ie converting an ac supply either to steady dc (with the aid of one or more capacitors) or to pulses of uniform polarity. The power supply used to enable an item of electronic equipment (such as an electronic controller) to be operated from an ac mains supply usually consists of a transformer which steps the high mains voltage down to a suitable voltage, say 16 V ac, one or more rectifier diodes and probably one or more electrolytic capacitors to help keep the resultant dc free from ripples and hums. For certain delicate electronic equipment a power supply may incorporate a voltage stabilising circuit employing voltage-reference diodes and a number of transistors possibly in an integrated circuit (a 'chip'), but such sophistication is unnecessary for normal model railway purposes.

The simplest circuit for converting the ac output from a mains transformer secondary to pulsed dc is shown in Figure A9.2; a single rectifier diode is connected in series with the transformer secondary. During that part of each positive-going half cycle when the voltage at A relative to that at B exceeds the offset voltage (0.7 V for a silicon diode), the diode will conduct. The output from this simple transformer/rectifier combination, as was stated, is not steady dc, but a series of pulses, known—for obvious reasons—as *rectified ac*. The reason for this is demonstrated in Figure A9.3. The output consists, to all intents and purposes, of alternate half cycles of ac. Such recitification in which only half of the available ac waveform is utilised is called *half-wave rectification*.

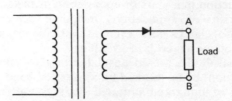

Figure A9.2 *The simplest possible transformer rectifier circuit.*

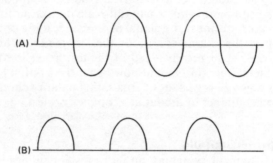

Figure A9.3 *Waveforms of (a) ac mains supply and (b) half-wave rectifier ac as obtained at the output of the circuit in Figure A9.2.*

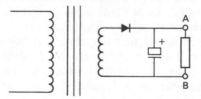

Figure A9.4 *The circuit of Figure A9.2 with a smoothing capacitor added.*

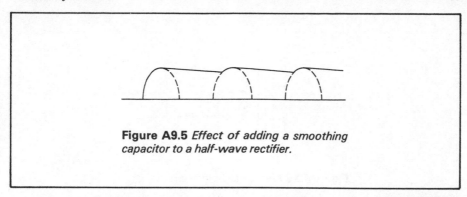

Figure A9.5 *Effect of adding a smoothing capacitor to a half-wave rectifier.*

The voltage output from such a half-wave rectifier circuit will be lower than one might expect. If the transformer in Figure A9.2 delivers 16 V ac (the actual peak excursions being around ± 23 V), the output from the rectifier as measured on a dc volt meter is likely to be around 7.3 V, this representing the rms figure divided by two (since only half the 'waves' are used) less the offset voltage of 0.7 V (a silicon rectifier is assumed). Nevertheless within this indicated 7.3 V there are peaks of over 22 V and if used as a power supply for an electronic controller almost certainly a better performance will be obtained than from a power supply which delivered a steady 7.3 V dc. The reasons for this are given in Project 8.

Some electronic circuits, including some types of electronic controller, operate well from a pulsed power supply such as that described above. Others, however, must have a smooth, continuous dc supply. One way of obtaining a smooth dc output from the circuit shown in Figure A9.2 is to add a *smoothing* capacitor across its output terminals, giving the circuit shown in Figure A9.4. If the same transformer is used that was described in the last paragraph, we should be perhaps surprised to find that adding the capacitor raises the indicated voltage on a dc voltmeter across the output from 7.3 V to around 22 V! It should not surprise us really—the new reading represents the *peaks* of excursion of the ac in the transformer secondary. Each peak of input causes the capacitor to charge up to that voltage. The capacitor discharges comparatively slowly through the output load and so most of that peak voltage is retained between cycles; any diminution in voltage is replenished at the next peak; this is shown in Figure A9.5, which demonstrates how much 'smoother' the output has become. The rate of discharge of the capacitor (indicated by the gently falling slope between cycles in Figure A9.5) is determined by the load, ie, the resistance of the circuit being driven, and by the value of the smoothing capacitor. Obviously the lower the resistance or the smaller the capacitor, the more rapidly it will discharge, resulting in a lower mean output voltage. In practice the minimum value of capacitor that will maintain an adequate average supply voltage is chosen. For many electronics applications this will be a high-value electrolytic type, eg 1,000 μF.

Full-wave rectification

Another way of obtaining a smoother power supply is to arrange for both positive- and negative-going half cycles of ac to be combined to give pulses of uniform polarity. One way of achieving this is shown in Figure A9.6, in which

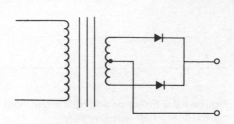

Figure A9.6 *Full-wave rectifier circuit.*

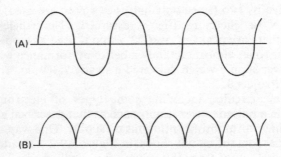

Figure A9.7 *Waveform of (a) ac mains supply and (b) full-wave rectifier ac.*

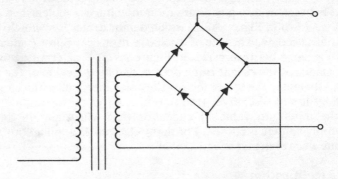

Figure A9.8 *Bridge rectifier circuit.*

the transformer secondary has a centre tap. The two diodes conduct alternately so that the ac output of the transformer becomes full-wave rectified ac; see Figure A9.7 for its waveform. One type of electronic controller (described in Projects 9 and 10) depends for correct operation on a rectified ac power supply having this waveform. A dc voltmeter across the output of the circuit shown in Figure A9.6 would indicate around 16 V dc if the transformer secondary were rated 16 V ac. For some electronics applications a smoothing capacitor would still be needed (as otherwise there are still two instants in each ac cycle when the output of this circuit is zero; this will upset some circuits, such as bistables). A capacitor across the output of the 16 V circuit described will raise its output voltage to around 22 V, as in the half-wave rectifier circuit.

An alternative method of obtaining full-wave rectification, in which a centre-tapped secondary is not needed, is to use what is known as a *bridge rectifier circuit*; a typical example is shown in Figure A9.8. Opposite pairs of diodes conduct alternately, the output waveform being identical to that of the circuit shown in Figure A9.6. Output voltage, however, will be very slightly less, because the current must always pass through two diodes and therefore two doses of offset voltage must be subtracted. Nevertheless the bridge rectifier is one of the commonest rectifier configurations. It may be made up from four separate diodes or from one four-terminal device containing the four silicon junctions.

Voltage doubler

Consider again the smoothed half-wave rectifier circuit shown in Figure A9.4; remember that the diode conducts, charging the capacitor, during positive-going half cycles of input only. Now imagine a second diode being added to the circuit with its cathode to the anode of the first diode and a second capacitor from its anode to 'ground' providing a second output. The circuit is shown in Figure A9.9. This second diode will clearly conduct only on negative-going half cycles of input and its output voltage relative to 'ground' will clearly by analogy with the first diode be around -22 V. So now we have a three-terminal output: the terminals offer + 22 V, 0 V and -22 V. For certain types of electronic controller such a symmetrical power supply is very useful. If we measure the PD from the + 22-V terminal to the -22-V terminal, we find of course that it is 22 (-22) V = 44 V. The 22 V nominal supply has been effectively doubled, hence the name of this type of circuit. Note that if the capacitors were removed no voltage doubling would occur; the diodes would conduct alternately providing half-wave rectified ac on either 'live' output terminal, but never on both simultaneously. This, too, can be useful and a controller using such a power supply is described in Project 8.

Diodes as voltage stabilisers

The voltage/current relationship for a silicon junction was given in Figure A9.1. Examination of this reveals that over a wide range of forward currents the PD across a silicon junction approximates to 0.7 V, its offset voltage. This means that a forward-biased diode can be used as a *voltage reference*, ie, as a stable source of a known voltage. The current passing through may be subject to fluctuations, but the voltage should remain fairly constant. Arrays of diodes in series could be used to provide any reference voltage that is a multiple of 0.7 V; Figure A9.10 shows how eight such diodes could be used to

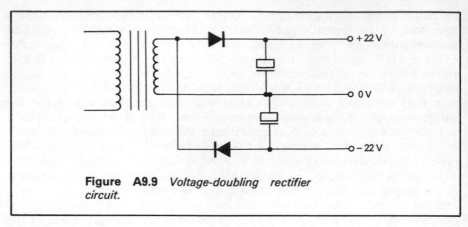

Figure A9.9 *Voltage-doubling rectifier circuit.*

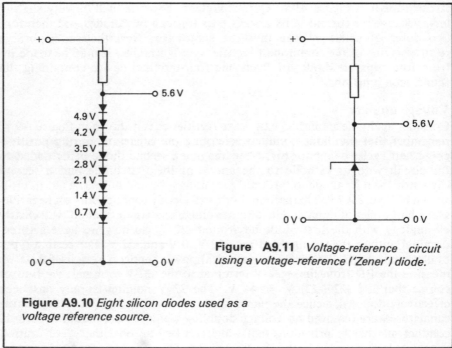

Figure A9.11 *Voltage-reference circuit using a voltage-reference ('Zener') diode.*

Figure A9.10 *Eight silicon diodes used as a voltage reference source.*

provide a reference source of 5.6 V. Such an array, however, is clumsy and in practice would be replaced by one 'Zener' diode for the required voltage— Figure A9.11. Such a voltage-reference diode is reverse-biased and operates under controlled breakdown conditions.

Appendix 10: Transistors

Transistors are divided into several classes of which just two will be considered in this book: *bipolar transistors* (usually called simply 'transistors') and *field-effect transistors* (usually called FETs or even 'fets' rhyming with 'nets'). Of the two, bipolar transistors are more useful to the railway modeller; only occasionally will the peculiar properties of FETs come to the aid of the railway modeller with an electronics problem.

The operation of bipolar transistors

A junction diode consists of one pn junction; a bipolar transistor consists of two. It has either two regions of n-type conductivity separated by a very thin layer of a p-type material or two regions of p-type material separated by a thin layer of n-type. For obvious reasons such transistors are referred to as npn and pnp respectively. The mode of operation is identical for both, but all the polarities concerned are, of course, reversed. The chemistry of silicon is such that it favours the production of npn devices, although silicon pnp types are by no means uncommon and many circuits demand the use of both.

The thin layer at the centre of the transistor is called the *base*; the other two zones are called the *collector* and the *emitter*. Connections are made to each. The symbols for npn and pnp transistors are shown in Figure A10.1. Note that the polarity of the device represented is indicated by the direction of the arrow on the emitter; this points in the direction of conventional current flow.

Consider an npn transistor connected to a 9 V battery *via* a milliameter as shown in Figure A10.2. The base is connected via an 82 K current-limiting resistor to a changeover switch by which it can be connected to either the positive or the negative terminal of the battery; we begin with it connected to the negative side of the battery. The milliameter will indicate no current (except for a leakage current so tiny that for practical purposes it may generally be ignored). It is not hard to see why this should be so. The collector-base junction is reverse biased and behaves like a reverse-biased diode. The base-emitter junction is effectively unbiased. Both junctions are virtually non-conductive.

If we throw the switch so that the base is connected to the *positive* side of the battery via the 82 K resistor, the transistor will behave very differently. The base-emitter junction is now forward-biased; consequently the pd across it will be around 0.7 V and the current flowing in the base circuit can be calculated by Ohm's law as (9.0-0.7) V/82 K = 0.1 mA (approximately). Our milliameter will now indicate that a very much larger current is also flowing in the collector circuit, even though the collector-base junction is supposedly reverse-biased; for a high-grade transistor a typical collector current under these conditions would be 20 mA (showing a current gain of 20/0.1 = 200), although this varies widely, even among devices of nominally the same type. This collector current is stimulated by the base current and will stop as soon as the base current is stopped, eg, by throwing back the switch in the circuit of Figure A10.2. So a small base current (0.1 mA in our example) is seen to control a much larger collector current (20 mA in our example).

When the base-emitter junction is forward-biased, electrons flow from the n-region (the emitter) across the junction and into the p-region (the base). But the base is a very thin region so that these electrons are bound to pass very close to the collector-base junction. Although there is around the collector-base junction—as around any reverse-biased junction—a depletion area, its extent is limited by the thinness of the base and this, together with the powerful attraction of the positive potential on the collector, ensures that *most of the electrons crossing the base-emitter junction reach the collector*. Only a

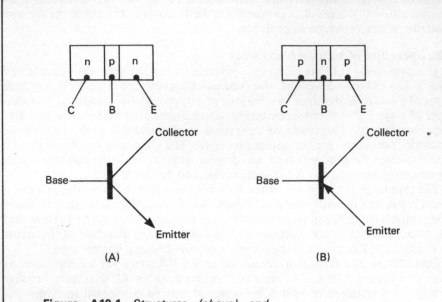

Figure A10.1 *Structures (above) and symbols (below) for (a) an npn transistor and (b) a pnp transistor.*

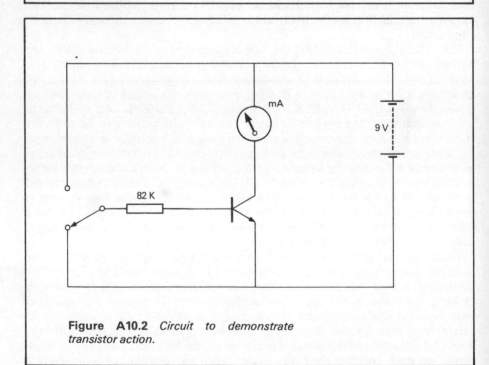

Figure A10.2 *Circuit to demonstrate transistor action.*

minority actually emerge on the base terminal. Consequently the small base current is capable of controlling the much larger collector current. In some transistors under favourable conditions the current amplification factor may be as high as 500, ie,

$$I_c = 500 I_b$$

where I_c is the collector current and I_b the base current. The current gain (I_c/I_b) of any transistor, however, is not constant, but varies with collector current. It is obvious that:

$$I_e = I_b + I_c$$

where I_e is emitter current.

Biasing of transistors

To employ a transistor in a circuit correctly it is, of course, necessary to ensure that the base-emitter junction is suitably forward-biased and the collector-base is suitably reverse-biased. As a very general guide a transistor is connected as shown in Figure A10.3. Resistor R_e in the emitter circuit is clearly common to both base and collector current and acts as a feedback loop to stabilise the collector current. Since the base current is negligible compared to the collector current, we may say that by Ohm's law:

$$V_e = I_c R_e$$

But V_e is determined by V_b; since the base-emitter junction is forward-biased:

$$V_e = V_b - 0.7$$

(a silicon transistor is assumed) and, since I_b is small compared with the current flowing in the potential divider R_{b1} and R_{b2}, V_b is fixed by the potential divider (or any other source of potential on the base).

We can see now how the current regulation mechanism works. If the collector current should fall, V_e must fall (by Ohm's law), but V_b stays constant. So the pd across the base-emitter junction will become greater than 0.7 V, significantly increasing the base current. This in turn will bring about a significant increase in collector current. Should the collector current rise too high V_e will also rise (by Ohm's law) and the PD across the base-emitter junction will become less than 0.7 V, significantly reducing the base current. This in turn will reduce the collector current. So, substituting for V_e in the two equations above:

$$I_c = \frac{V_b - 0.7}{R_e}$$

The collector current may be said, therefore, to be determined by the base voltage and the emitter resistance. A change in either will alter the collector current. For this reason both base and emitter are said to present a low input resistance.

However the collector resistance, R_c, is different. Its value has no effect on the collector current provided, of course, that it is not made so great that the supply voltage cannot (by Ohm's law) drive the collector current through it. The voltage on the collector will be the supply voltage less the PD across the collector load resistor. Even changing the supply voltage will not affect the

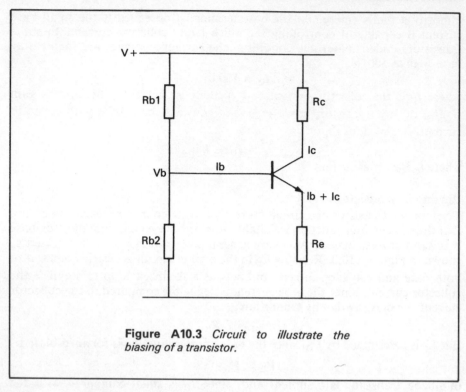

Figure A10.3 *Circuit to illustrate the biasing of a transistor.*

collector current, provided the base voltage is constant. Consequently the collector is said to have a high output resistance.

It was said earlier that a transistor's input consists of a base *current*. Then reference was made to as base *voltage*. In Figure A10.3 the base of the transistor is connected to a potential divider, essentially a voltage source. The base current is often so small that the base input resistance can be regarded as high. This can be seen if we take the circuit of Figure A10.3 and assign values to the components, as shown in Figure A10.4.

We shall assume that the base input resistance is so high compared with the 33 K lower arm of the potential divider that it does not significantly affect the operation of the potential divider; shortly we shall demonstrate that this is indeed so. So the voltage on the base of the transistor is determined purely by the potential divider as:

$$\frac{33 \times 12}{33 + 68} = 4.0 \text{ V appx}$$

Therefore the voltage on the emitter is 4.0-0.7 = 3.3 V. Since this voltage is applied across the 3.3 K emitter resistor, the collector current is stabilised at 3.3 V/3.3 K = 1 mA. The PD across the 6.8 K collector load resistor is therefore:

$$1 \text{ mA} \times 6.8 \text{ K} = 6.8 \text{ V}$$

and the voltage on the collector (relative to the negative line) is 12.0-6.8 = 5.2 V.

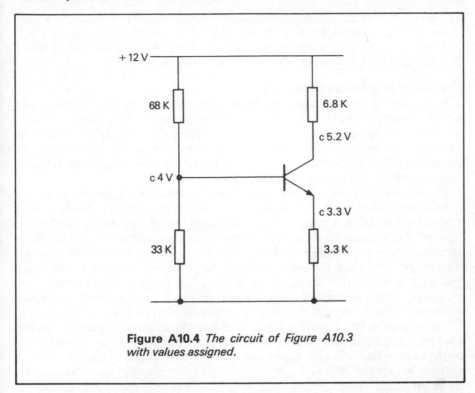

Figure A10.4 *The circuit of Figure A10.3 with values assigned.*

We can see now that a transistor is capable of giving voltage gain besides current gain. If the base voltage were to fall from 4.0 V to 2.4 V, the emitter voltage would now be 2.4-0.7 = 1.7 V, the collector current 1.7/3.3 = 0.5 mA (approximately), the PD across the collector load 0.5 × 6.8 = 3.4 V and the collector voltage would *rise* from 5.2 V to 12.0-3.4 = 8.6 V. Thus a change of 1.6 V on the base causes a change of 3.4 V on the collector. This is only a doubling of 'signal voltage'; far greater voltage amplification can be achieved if required.

However, transistors primarily give *current amplification*; the base *current* controls the collector *current*. Indeed, the voltage amplification just described is simply a side effect of the current amplification. If the current gain of the transistor in the circuit of Figure 4.4 were 200 at a collector current of 1 mA, the base current under those conditions would be 1/200 mA = 5 µA. We can now calculate the base input resistance. Since a base voltage of 4.0 V drives a base current of 5 µA, the input resistance is:

$$\frac{4.0 \text{ V}}{5 \text{ µA}} = 0.8 \text{ M}\Omega \text{ (or 800 K)}$$

This is indeed high compared with the lower arm of the potential divider (33 K) and therefore does not significantly affect its voltage output. It is, however, important always to ensure that any resistors in the base circuit of a transistor are *low* compared to the input resistance.

If in the circuit of Figure A10.4 the collector of the transistor were disconnected, transistor action would cease and the base-emitter junction would function as an ordinary silicon diode. The 33 K resistor would now have in parallel the equivalent of a forward-biased diode in series with a 3.3 K resistor. This is equivalent to about an 8 K resistor in parallel with the 33 K and the output of the potential divider would fall to about 1 V.

Transistor amplifying circuits

A transistor, as we have seen, has three terminals. The input circuit uses two and the output circuit uses two. It follows that one terminal is always common to input and output circuits. There are, in fact, three kinds of amplifying circuit: common-collector (more generally known as emitter follower), common-emitter and common-base amplifiers, depending upon the terminal that is common to input and output circuits.

The *emitter follower* is the simplest kind of transistor amplifying stage and is frequently used in model railway electronics; a simplified diagram of a typical emitter follower stage is shown in Figure A10.5. Input is applied to the base of the transistor and output taken from the emitter. The collector is effectively 'grounded' and therefore is common to input and output. There is no voltage gain, since the output voltage must always be equal to the input voltage less 0.7 V (for a silicon transistor), but there is current gain. The transistor might perhaps be the output stage of an electronic controller delivering 250 mA controlled by a base current of, say, 10 mA.

The emitter follower offers high input resistance (current gain × emitter load resistance) and low output resistance, since any changes in the resistance of the emitter load will affect the biasing of the transistor and thus the emitter current. An emitter-follower output stage in a controller will show 'sensitivity' to motor back EMF which will help to improve speed regulation. A disadvantage of the emitter follower as an output stage is that, while the output voltage can be reduced to zero by bringing the base voltage down to zero (or near it), the output voltage can never equal the full supply voltage, since, even if the base voltage is raised to the supply voltage, the output from the emitter will still be 0.7 V lower.

The *common-emitter* stage closely resembles the emitter follower, as a comparison of Figure A10.6 with Figure A10.5 will show. The principal difference is in the placing of the load. In the emitter follower this was common to input and output circuits, reducing voltage gain to unity. In the common-emitter stage there is no such limit to voltage gain. Indeed the way in which such a circuit gives voltage gain was described earlier when we were considering bias. We noticed that collector voltage *rises* as base voltage *falls*; conversely, of course, collector voltage will fall as base voltage rises. The output voltage is therefore said to be *antiphase* with input voltage.

Like the emitter follower, a common-emitter stage gives current gain, the current output rising as the base voltage (and current) rise. As an output stage a common-emitter amplifier has an advantage over an emitter follower in that the full power-supply voltage is available: collector voltage will equal power supply voltage when the base bias is zero (and the transistor is not conducting) but can also fall to equal the emitter voltage when sufficient current flows through the collector load; interestingly, when this happens both junctions in the transistor are simultaneously forward biased and the transistor is then said to be operating under *saturation conditions*. Since the collector presents a high output resistance, this kind of amplifier circuit does not exhibit the same kind

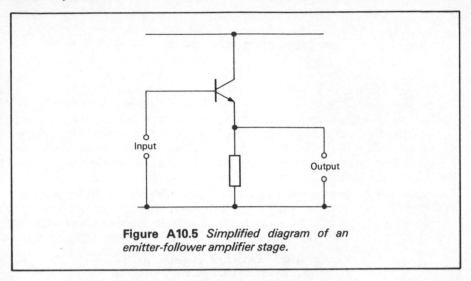

Figure A10.5 *Simplified diagram of an emitter-follower amplifier stage.*

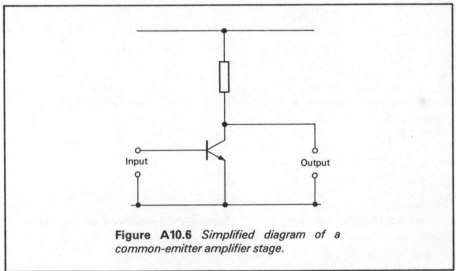

Figure A10.6 *Simplified diagram of a common-emitter amplifier stage.*

of 'sensitivity' to changes in the output conditions as does an emitter follower. In a practical multi-stage circuit, however, such 'sensitivity' can be provided, if required, by a separate feedback loop to an earlier stage.

The *common-base* amplifier is rarely used in model railway electronics; T1 in Figure 17.1 (EDOTIS) is an interesting example. As Figure A10.7 shows, input is applied to the emitter and taken from the collector, the base being common. We have already noticed that the emitter, like the base, is sensitive to changes in operating conditions. Since the collector current is nearly equal to the emitter current (the difference being the almost negligible base current), there can be no current gain. However, there is voltage gain; since effectively the same current flows in R_e and R_c, it follows that the voltage gain equals R_c/R_e. Since a positive-going bias on the emitter is equivalent to a negative-

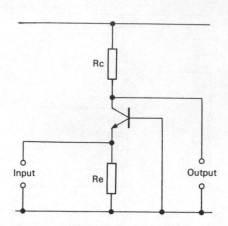

Figure A10.7 *Simplified diagram of a common-base amplifier stage.*

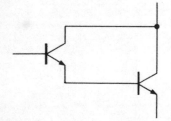

Figure A10.8 *Darlington pair.*

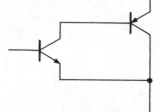

Figure A10.9 *Modified Darlington pair.*

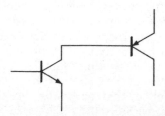

Figure A10.10 *The circuit of Figure A10.9 with the feedback path removed.*

going bias on the base, this will decrease collector current and *raise* collector voltage. Thus, unlike that given by a common-emitter stage, this voltage gain is in phase with the input. Since the output is taken from the collector, it shows the same high output resistance as does a common-emitter stage.

Summary table of characteristics of transistor amplifier stages

Type	Emitter follower	Common emitter	Common base
Input between	base and collector	base and emitter	emitter and base
Output between	emitter and collector	collector and emitter	collector and base
Input resistance	high	medium	low
Output resistance	low	high	high
Voltage gain	unity (less offset)	high	high
Current gain	high	high	unity (less base current)
Output voltage relative to input voltage	in phase	antiphase	in phase

Direct coupling of transistors

In many applications—and especially in electronic controllers—it is essential to cascade two or more transistors, ie, they must be connected so that all (or most) of the output of the first transistor is used as the input for the second transistor and similarly all (or most) of the output of the second transistor is used as the input for the third transistor if used. Since current output is available from both the collector and base of a transistor and devices of either polarity must be used, there are a number of ways in which two transistors may be coupled.

Figure A10.8 shows what is known as a *Darlington pair*. The two collectors are bonded and the emitter current of the first transistor is the base bias of the second. It has the advantages of very high input resistance and of high efficiency: even the collector current of the first transistor forms part of the output current. Output may be taken from the collectors or the emitter of the second transistor; if the latter, there will, of course, be no voltage gain. The Darlington pair may be regarded as one compound transistor having very high current gain.

Figure A10.9 shows a modified Darlington circuit in which the second transistor is of opposite polarity to the first. Output would normally be taken from the collector of the second transistor, which is also the emitter of the first. Because the output load is also part of the emitter circuit of the first transistor, this circuit exhibits a remarkable ability to compensate for changes in load. It is incapable of providing voltage gain therefore; it behaves like an emitter follower having very high current gain.

The configuration shown in Figure A10.10 resembles the previous one except that the feedback path between the output and the emitter of the first transistor has been removed. Output may be taken from the collector of the second transistor, where there will be both high voltage gain and high current gain; output voltage will be in phase with input, since phase is inverted twice, the circuit being essentially two common-emitter stages in cascade. Alternatively output may be taken from the emitter of the second transistor, where there will be moderate voltage gain and high current gain; output will be antiphase with input, having been inverted in the first transistor.

The circuit shown in Figure A10.11 is known rather quaintly as a *long-tailed* pair. It resembles two stages of common-emitter amplification having a common emitter resistor. Indeed, if either transistor is left without an input on its base, the other will function as a normal common-emitter stage. The emitter coupling ensures that signals applied to the base of T 1 also appear at the emitter of T 2, which now functions as a *common-base* amplifier. Thus any signal applied to input 1 will give an antiphase amplified voltage output from the collector of T 1 and a similar but in-phase output at the collector of T 2. Since the circuit is symmetrical a similar result will be obtained by applying a signal to input 2. If identical signals are applied to both inputs, in theory they cancel each other giving zero output. A long-tailed pair is sometimes used for comparing two voltages; in an electronic controller, for instance, it could be used to compare the controller output with a control voltage.

Field-effect transistors

A field-effect transistor (FET) is a semi-conductor amplifying device working on principles quite different from those of bipolar transistors and consequently having somewhat different characteristics. The properties of FETs, however, render them rather less useful to the railway modeller than are bipolar transistors, so that they are likely to be encountered only in certain specialist applications (see Project 31). Perhaps the greatest importance of FETs is their application in many integrated circuits ('chips'), such as COS/MOS types, which are beyond the scope of this book. Consequently, although FETs are a very much more diverse group of devices than bipolar transistors (and represented by a corresponding diversity of diagrammatic symbols), there is no need for the railway modeller to master them all; the junction-gate types will suffice.

The free electrons and holes in n-type and p-type silicon respectively make these materials fair conductors of electricity in contrast with pure silicon. If electrical connections are made to each end of a strip of, say, n-type silicon, it will behave as a linear resistor, ie, current may flow in either direction and will be proportional to the EMF applied.

Now imagine that a zone of p-type material encircles our strip of n-type material like a belt and forms a circular junction with it. If a connection is made to the p-type zone, we have a three-terminal device. If no bias is applied to the p-type zone, the strip will continue to show normal, linear conductivity. If *reverse* bias is applied to the junction, ie, the p-region is made negative relative to the n-type strip, a depletion zone will be established in the strip making it effectively narrower and therefore increasing its resistance. If the reverse bias is made greater, the depletion zone will constrict the conductive region of the strip even more, making it even more resistant. If the reverse bias is great enough, the depletion zone will spread right across the strip cutting off current altogether; the device is now said to be 'pinched off'. Thus a current is being controlled by a voltage applied across a reverse-biased junction. This type of device is called a *junction-gate FET* (JUGFET or JFET).

The normally-conductive strip is called the *channel*; if it is of n-type material, the device is said to be *n-channel* (cf npn); if it is of p-type material, the device is said to be *p-channel* (cf pnp). The terminals at the ends of the

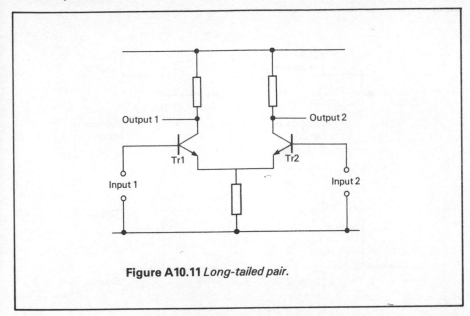

Figure A10.11 *Long-tailed pair.*

channel are called the *source* (corresponding to the emitter) and the *drain* (corresponding to the collector). The control terminal connected to the other side of the junction is called the *gate* (and corresponds to the base). Many JUGFETs, including the types most likely to be encountered in model railway applications, are electrically symmetrical, the drain and source terminals being interchangeable. Because of this there are four symbols for JUGFETs as shown in Figure A10.12.

At once several practical differences between the operation of JUGFETs and bipolar transistors are apparent:

i) An unbiased JUGFET is conductive, reverse bias being applied to control the drain current by reducing it; it is known as *depletion-mode* operation. In contrast, an unbiased bipolar transistor is non-conductive, forward bias being needed to establish collector current; this is known as *enhancement-mode* operation.

ii) A JUGFET will conduct current in either direction (hence the reversibility of symmetrical types), whereas a bipolar transistor will not function normally with collector and emitter leads interchanged.

iii) The gate input resistance of a JUGFET under normal conditions is that of a reverse-biased pn junction and for practical purposes may be regarded as infinite. Input current is infinitesimal; the input signal may be regarded as an electrostatic charge.

As with bipolar transistors current is stabilised by a resistor in series with the source and by returning the gate to a fixed potential, often the most negative point in the circuit (an n-channel device is assumed). There can be no set formula for determining the drain current; this is best found by experiment. Amplifier circuits having common-drain (source follower), common-source and common-gate configurations are all possible; the following table summarises their characteristics.

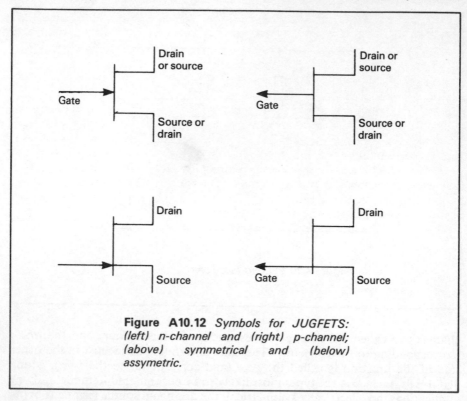

Figure A10.12 *Symbols for JUGFETS: (left) n-channel and (right) p-channel; (above) symmetrical and (below) assymetric.*

Summary table of characteristics of FET amplifier stages

Type	Source follower	Common source	Common gate
Input between	gate and drain	gate and source	source and gate
Output between	source and drain	drain and source	drain and gate
Input resistance	infinite	infinite	low
Output resistance	low	high	high
Voltage gain	unity	medium	medium
Current gain	infinite*	infinite*	unity
Output voltage relation to input voltage	in phase	antiphase	in phase

*Current gain must be regarded as infinite since input current is zero (input resistance being infinite) but output current is finite.

Appendix 11: Suggested further reading

Electronics in general

Thousands of books have been written on electronics. They cater for all tastes from hobbyists to post-doctoral researchers. A visit to a good reference library should enable the reader to sample a selection of them. Out of hundreds worthy of mention and which could be useful to readers of this book wanting more detailed information, here are three with which the author is familiar and to which he is happy to acknowledge his gratitude for help.

Foundations of Wireless and Electronics by M.G. Scroggie (Butterworths). Generations have learned electronics from Scroggie. Over the years the book has grown (even its title has—it used to be just *Foundations of Wireless*) with the subject. No prior knowledge is needed. The book deals comprehensively and in an entertaining manner with a broad diversity of subjects. Nevertheless the approach is theoretical rather than practical.

Principles of Transistor Circuits by S.W. Amos (Butterworths). More specialised than Scroggie, this book deals in greater depth with the operation of semi-conductor devices and circuits employing them. Hardly a book for the casual experimenter, but those wishing to master the subject will find their understanding clarified; readers may also find suggestions to the solution of problems. Knowledge of the basic principles is assumed.

The Art of Electronics by P. Horowitz and W. Hill (Cambridge University Press). An unusual book combining theoretical and practical content; like Scroggie it assumes no prior knowledge, but it also includes such details as data for popular devices and suggested circuits. Humorous in style, the book even includes 'bad circuits' guaranteed not to work but included to test the reader's skill in spotting design faults. Since the book was written primarily for the US market the devices mentioned are mainly US types, some of which may be hard to find elsewhere.

Model railway electronics

Following are details of the only other books on this subject (or relevant to it) that the author has found. Most demand some prior knowledge of electronics fundamentals, but those who have read this book should have little difficulty with them. The last three came to the author's attention only after he had finished writing most of this book, hence the absence from these pages of certain techniques taken for granted in the USA.

Simple Electronics for Modellers by Ian R. Sinclair (Model and Allied Publications). As its title suggests, this book is intended for modellers in general, not only railway modellers. For a book claiming to be 'simple' its content is surprisingly theoretical, with chapters devoted to generating signals and delays, electronic measurements, counting circuits and logic circuits. It may give the railway modeller a few ideas, but otherwise its main appeal is its advocacy of popular integrated circuits (deliberately omitted from the present book for simplicity). Even so, some explanation of how the ics work would have been helpful. Printed circuit board layouts are given for each project described.

Electronic Circuits for Model Railways by M.H. Babani (Bernard Babani). A collection of articles reprinted from an Australian magazine. The projects described include controllers (some with inertia simulation), interlock systems (to stop trains at signals, etc), coach lighting and sound effects. There is a useful chapter on radio interference suppression. The coach lighting system is most interesting: Babani rejected a high-frequency system because, he says, it was too complex, the locomotives required modification and it interfered with signalling systems—the present author experienced no such difficulties! Babani's coach lighting system uses rechargeable cells carried in the train and switched using train-mounted reed switches operated by track-mounted magnets. Babani sccms inordinately fond of relays when semi-conductor bistables would do the job equally well and more cheaply. When Babani refers to 'automatic signalling' he means the automatic stopping and starting of trains at manually operated signals. Nevertheless there is useful material here.

Model Railway Projects by R.A. Penfold (Bernard Babani). Like M.H. Babani's book (above), which this replaces, some familiarity with electronics is assumed. Presentation is greatly improved and the projects updated, some using ics and one even using power MOSFETs. Gone is Babani's unique coach lighting system and the chapter on interference suppression. Included is an automatic unidirectional signalling system using magnet/reed switch train detection, but why the author has chosen to use power MOSFETs in his bistable when bipolar transistors would work just as well at one tenth the cost is hard to imagine; if he is afraid that the bias current will set the 'off' LED glowing, the simple solution is to connect a suitable resistor (often 1.5 K) in parallel with it. Also included are controllers, turnout operation, signal interlocks and sound effects.

Model Railroad Electonics by James Kyle (Tab Books, Blue Ridge Summit, USA, distributed in the UK by W. Foulsham & Co Ltd, Slough). A delightful book written for the US market, but equally relevant to UK readers. The range of topics covered is limited: coach lighting and sound effects are omitted; but what is included—controllers, train detection, signalling—is covered in considerable depth. The approach is somewhat theoretical, despite a section on tools and soldering, and the reader is left to himself to select semi-conductors of suitable rating for the projects described. Perhaps this is just as well, for if US types had been specified these might be hard to locate else-where. The author uses digital techniques and ics galore and much that is included is highly sophisticated. Indeed, in places he is tantalising. He gives, for instance, a block diagram for a complex, high-performance controller, but not a full circuit diagram, thereby—despite having whetted the reader's appetite—withholding the opportunity to construct it. Later he gives a complete circuit diagram for a progressive cab control unit (a system which automatically 'hands the controller on' from section to section as the train progresses round the layout). This uses a large number of digital ics. Then he says that the whole circuit can be constructed using just a few lsi (large-scale integration) chips. But he does not say which chips, nor how to use them. These criticisms aside, Kyle is always witty and stimulating; you cannot read him without getting a 'mindful' of new ideas!

Practical Electronic Projects for Model Railroaders by Peter J. Thorne (Kalmbach Book, Milwaukee, Wisconsin, USA). Another excellent book from across the Atlantic. Magazine-type format has enabled the publisher to cram an enormous amount of information into a small number of pages. The book begins with fundamentals and proceeds to a range of projects including controllers, point motor ('switch machine' in US parlance) drivers, train detection (three systems), signalling systems (two- and three-aspect), sound effects including synchronised and on-train sound systems, coach lighting and loco lighting. If less detailed than Kyle, Thorne is more comprehensive in coverage and practical in approach. Full circuit diagrams, pcb layouts and component lists are given. Interestingly the author is a Canadian and he gives

Canadian semi-conductor equivalents to the US types specified in the components lists; these type numbers will be familiar to European readers! Like Kyle, this book will inspire the reader with new ideas and provide useful facts.

Index

Other PSL books for railway modellers

How To Go Railway Modelling
(4th edition)
by Norman Simmons
Now in its fourth, revised and updated edition to take account of the revolution
in microchip technology and other changes since the third edition was published
two years ago, this 'bible' of the railway modelling hobby is now even more
timely than ever before.

PSL Model Railway Guide series
by Michael Andress
1 *Baseboards, track and electrification;* **2** *Layout planning;* **3** *Structure modelling;*
4 *Scenery;* **5** *Operating your layout;* **6** *Branch line railways;* **7** *Modern railways;*
8 *Narrow-gauge railways.*
This series of eight inexpensive guides to the basics of good railway modelling is a
'must' for every newcomer to the hobby and will also give many ideas to old
hands.

PSL's Practical Guide to Railway Modelling
edited by Michael Andress
This good-value practical handbook comprises a variety of railway modelling
topics chosen to be of greatest use to the modeller with no special skill or
experience. All the features have been selected to cover the main aspects of
railway modelling—locomotives, passenger and goods rolling stock, special
equipment, operation, structures and scenery.

How To Go Tram & Tramway Modelling
by David Voice
This is the first full-length treatment of an increasingly popular aspect of the
modelling hobby. In clear text accompanied by numerous photographs and
diagrams, the author explains everything which the would-be tram modeller needs
to know, while long and detailed appendices provide a great deal of valuable
information not available anywhere else.

See also back jacket flap.